LAOTZU'S TAO
AND WU WEI

CONTENTS

LAOTZU' S TAO-TEH-KING

ESSAYS INTERPRETING TAOISM

HISTORICAL ESSAYS

INTRODUCTION

I LOVE LAOTZU! That is the reason I offer an-other interpretative translation, and try to print and bind it attractively. I want you to appreciate this wise and kindly old man, and come to love him. He was perhaps the first of scholars (6th century B.C.) to have a vision of spiritual reality, and he tried so hard to explain it to others, only, in the end, to wander away into the Great Unknown in pathetic discouragement. Everything was against him; his friends misunderstood him; others made fun of him.

Even the written characters which he must use to preserve his thought conspired against him. They were only five thousand in all, and were ill adapted to express mystical and abstract ideas. When these characters are translated accurately, the translation is necessarily awkward and obscure. Sinologues have unintentionally done him an injustice by their very scholarship. I have tried to peer through the clumsy characters into his heart and prayed that love for him would make me wise to understand aright.

I hate scholarship that would deny his existence, or arrogant erudition that says patronizingly, "Oh, yes, there doubtless was some one who wrote some of the characteristic sonnets, but most of them are an accumulation through the centuries of verses that have similar structure, and all have been changed and amended until it is better to call the book a collection of aphorisms."

Shame on scholarship when, sharing the visions of the illuminati, they deride them!

There are three great facts in China today that vouch for Laotzu. First, the presence of Taoism, which was suggested by his teachings, not founded upon them. This is explained by the inability of the scholars, who immediately followed him, to understand and appreciate the spirituality of his teachings. Second, Confucian dislike for Laotzian ideas, which is explained by their opposition to Confucian ethics. Third, and the greatest fact of all, is the characteristic traits of Chinese nature, namely, passivity, submissiveness and moral concern, all of which find an adequate cause and source in the teachings of Laotzu.

An interesting fact in regard to the thought of Laotzu is this. Although for two thousand years he has been misunderstood and derided, today the very best of scientific and philosophic thought, which gathers about what is known as Vitalism, is in full accord with Laotzu's idea of the Tao. Every reference that is made today to a Cosmic Urge, Vital Impulse, and Creative Principle can be said of the Tao. Everything that can be said of Plato's Ideas and Forms and of Cosmic Love as being the creative expression of God can be said of the Tao. When Christian scholars came to translate the Logos of St. John into Chinese, they were satisfied to use the word "Tao."

It is true that Laotzu's conception of the Tao was limited to a conception of a universal, creative principle. He apparently had no conception of personality, which the Christians ascribe to God, in connection with it, but he ascribed so much of wisdom and benevolence to it that his conception fell little short of personality. To Laotzu, the Tao is the universal and eternal principle which forms and conditions everything; it is that intangible cosmic influence which harmonizes all things and brings them to fruition; it is the norm and standard of truth and morality. Laotzu did more than entertain an intelligent opinion of Tao as a creative principle; he had a devout and religious sentiment towards it: "He loved the Tao as a son cherishes and reveres his mother."

There are three key words in the thought of Laotzu: Tao, Teh, and Wu Wei. They are all difficult to translate. The simple meaning of Tao is "way," but it also has a wide variety of other meanings. Dr. Paul Carus translates it, "Reason," but apologizes for so doing. If forced to offer a translation we would suggest Creative Principle, but much prefer to leave it untranslated.

The character, "Teh," is usually translated "virtue." This is correct as a mere translation of the character, but is in no sense adequate to the content of the thought in Laotzu's mind. To him, Teh meant precisely what is meant in the account of the healing of the woman who touched the hem of Jesus' robe: "Jesus was conscious that *virtue* had passed from him." Teh includes the meaning of vitality, of virility, of beauty and the harmony that we think of as that part of life that is abounding and joyous. The third word is the negative expression, "Wu Wei." Translated, this means "not acting," or "non-assertion." When Laotzu urges men to "wu wei," he is not urging them to laziness or asceticism. He means that all men are to cherish that wise humility and diffidence and selflessness which comes from a consciousness that the Tao is infinitely wise and good, and that the part of human wisdom is to hold one's self in such a restrained and receptive manner that the Tao may find one a suitable and conforming channel for its purpose. The title of Laotzu's book, Tao Teh King, is carelessly translated, The Way of Virtue Classic, or The Way and Virtue Classic. This is very inadequate. The Vitality of the Tao is very much better.

Most commentators think that Laotzu's teachings fit in especially well with Buddhist philosophy. This conclusion is arrived at by the common interpretation of wu wei as submission that will logically end in absorption of the spirit in Tao as Nirvana. This understanding of wu wei, which Henri Borel shares in a measure, is, we believe, incorrect, inasmuch as Laotzu consistently teaches a *finding* of life rather than a losing of it. Laotzu's conception of Tao as the underived Source of all things, finding expression through spiritual Teh in universal creative activity, is very close to Plato's doctrine of the good as the One ineffable Source of all things, whose Ideas and Forms of Goodness, Truth and Beauty radiated outward as spiritual logoi in creative activity through Spirit, Soul and Nature to the farthest confines of matter.

While it is true that Laotzu's teachings would find little in common with the Old Testament anthropomorphic autocracy, and would find almost nothing in common with the modern Ritschlean system of ethical idealism which has for its basis a naturalistic evolution of human society by means of philanthropy, laws, cultural civilizations, and human governments backed by force of arms, nevertheless his teachings are entirely in harmony with that Christian philosophy of the Logos, which is a heritage from the Greeks, through Plato, Philo, St. Paul, Plotinus, and Augustine, and which is the basis of the mystical faith of the Christian saints of all ages. While Laotzu would find little in common with the busy, impertinent activities of so-called Christian statesman building by statecraft and war, he would find much in common with Apostolic Christianity which held itself aloof from current politics and refused to enter the army, content to live simply, quietly, full of faith and humble benevolence.

And most of all would he find himself in sympathy with the teacher of Nazareth. At almost every Sonnet, one thinks of some corresponding expression of Jesus, who had a very similar conception of God, but who recognized in Him that personal element of Love which made God not only Creative Principle but Heavenly Father.

Laotzu's vision of the virile harmony, goodness, and Spirituality of the Tao was what Jesus saw as the Fatherhood of God, self-expressing his love-nature endlessly in all creative effort, and, through universal intuition, endlessly drawing his creation back to himself in grateful and humble affection. Laotzu saw in a glass darkly what Jesus saw face to face in all his glory, the Divine Tao, God as creative and redemptive Love.

As you read these verses, forget the words and phrases, poor material and poor workmanship at best, look through them for the soul of Laotzu. It is there revealed, but so imperfectly that it is only an apparition of a soul. But if by it, vague as it is, you come to love Laotzu, you will catch beyond him fleeting glimpses of the splendid visions that so possessed his soul, visions of Infinite Goodness, Humility and Beauty radiating from the Heart of creation.

DWIGHT GODDARD.

ALL WE KNOW ABOUT LAOTZU

SZE MA-CH'IEN (136-85 B.C.) wrote that Lao-tzu was born of the Li family of Ch'ujen Village, Li County, K'u Province, Ch'u State. His proper name was Err, his official name was Poh-yang, his posthumous title was Yueh-tan. He held the position of custodian of the secret archives of the State of Cheu.

Confucius went to Cheu to consult Laotzu about certain ceremonials; Laotzu told him: "The bones of these sages, concerning whom you inquire, have long since decayed, only their teachings remain. If a superior man is understood by his age, he rises to honor, but not being understood, his name is like a vagrant seed blown about by the wind. I have heard it said that a good merchant conceals his treasures, as though his warehouses were empty. The sage of highest worth assumes a countenance and outward mien as though he were stupid. Put aside your haughty airs, your many needs, affected robes and exaggerated importance. These add no real value to your person. That is my advice to you, and it is all I have to offer."

Confucius departed and when he later described to his students his visit to Laotzu, he said: "I understand about the habits of birds, how they can fly; how fish can swim; and animals run. For the running we can make snares, for the swimming we can make nets, for the flying we can make arrows. But for the dragon, I cannot know how he ascends on the winds and clouds to heaven. I have just seen Laotzu. Can it be said, he is as difficult to understand as the dragon? He teaches the vitality of Tao. His doctrine appears to lead one to aspire after self-effacement and obscurity."

Laotzu lived in Cheu for a long time; he prophesied the decay of that state and in consequence was obliged to depart, and went to the frontier. The officer at the border post was Yin-hi, who said to Laotzu, "If you are going to leave us, will you not write a book by which we may remember you?" Thereupon Laotzu wrote a book of sonnets in two parts, comprising in all about five thousand characters. In this book he discussed his conception of the Vitality of the Tao. He left this book with the soldier, and departed, no one knows whither.

INTRODUCTION TO SECOND EDITION

When the first edition was published in 1919, the writer was a Christian and had very little first hand acquaintance with Taoism. Since then he has become a Buddhist and by frequent visits to China has been studying Buddhism and Taoism for twelve years. The present translation was made by a Taoist-Buddhist monk, named Wai-tao (King Yun-pen) . He is about fifty years of age, learned English as a boy in a Mission Academy, and later graduated from the Department of Chinese Philosophy in the National University in Peiping. Soon after graduation he became a member of a Taoist-Buddhist Brotherhood and remained with them for many years until he left to enter the great Kwei-tsung Buddhist Monastery. After he had remained with them for three years, he returned to his earlier home with the Taoist-Buddhist Brotherhood. The writer visited him at his hermitage in the mountains of Southern Chekiang Province in the winter 1935 and remained with him for a number of weeks going over this translation of Laotzu's *Tao-teh-king* and two other translations.

The present translation is nearly double the length of the Chinese text, not because it is expanded by interpretation, but because it is necessary to do so in order to bring out the meaning of the five thousand ideographs which make up the text. Even when Chinese classical texts are transliterated into the colloquial the text is extended fifty percent and Laotzu's text is exceptionally condensed until it is almost cryptic in places. The translator had the use of a number of Taoist commentaries and was able to consult with a number of living Taoist masters. There are hundreds of these commentaries extant and many of them, in fact most of them, are exceedingly cryptic owing to the Taoist habit of expressing their teachings in secret symbols. The commentary which Wai-tao most consulted was a famous one entitled: *Tao-teh-king-ching-chu-chieh*. It is based upon the "divine elucidation" given to two great masters through the planchette.

The Tao conception is the most inclusive and concise conception in human thought, if not the grandest also. The Christian conception of God must be supplemented by doctrines and dogmas; the Buddhist conception of Buddhahood must be elucidated by other profound conceptions, such as, Dharmakaya, Sambhogakaya, Prajna, Tathata and Tathagata; but the Tao conception is self-contained, all-embracing, profound and inscrutable. It is, just as it is. "How do I know this? Because of Tao."

Arthur Waley in his recent scholarly study of Laotzu and this *Tao-teh-king* translates the title, The Way and its Power. (George Allen & Unwin Inc., London) . He speaks of Tao as the Principle of Naturalism which is excellent, but by seeking to crowd the book into a preconceived idea of its place in literary history, he makes the translation pedantic and disappointing. His painstaking study of its authorship is also unconvincing. Even if there was three Laos to whom the book has been credited (Laotzu, Lao Lai Tzu, and Lao Tan), who lived a total of perhaps two hundred years apart, there is no good reason why he should credit the book to the last, in the face of the almost universal Taoist belief that it was the original teaching of Laotzu. It is probably true that the Lao Tan in his teachings used earlier material, and if the book was not put into its final form until his time, it is more natural to think of Lao Tan as an editor, than it is to eliminate the earlier Laotzu, as does Waley. Moreover, Taoists universally believe that Laotzu and Lao Tan are the same person; in fact, there is some evidence that there was an earlier Lao Tan and that he was the same man as Laotzu. Admitted, it is a puzzling question but the general belief, in this is worthy of respect and confidence.

The London modernist and "higher critic" asserts that the book is a product of the Third Century by a Taoist politician combatting the

Confucian and political realism of his day. Opposed to this I would like to offer another hypothesis. Shakyamuni Buddha lived in India at about the same time that Laotzu is credited with living in China. (Buddha, 544-463 B.C. Laotzu.)

Waley thinks that the writing, *Tao-teh-king,* was put into its final form about 240 B.C. That it was in the main the writing of an unknown political realist, who wove into it earlier Taoist mysticism and metaphysics. Then he inclines to the belief that this unknown writer was a certain 4th Century official named Lao Tan. But there is a persistent belief that there was another Lao Tan who lived a century or two earlier and is credited as being the same person as the official Laotzu commonly called "the old Philosopher." This leaves a gap of some two hundred years during which certain Taoist writings had been increasingly credited to "the old philosopher," *i.e.* Laotzu.

The hypothesis I venture to suggest is this:—That the teachings of the Indian Shakyamuni Buddha had percolated into China during those two hundred years, being carried by travelling merchants and scholars. These Buddhist teachings being unwritten in those early days were necessarily carried in memory and became more or less confused and distorted, but as they blended easily with the current Taoist *philosophy*, they were commonly accepted and more or less kept together, and credited to "the old philosopher," Laotzu. This hypothesis explains the vagueness and confusion as to authorship and also the affinity of Laotzuan ideas with Buddhist thought. This hypothesis may seem fantastic to some but it is no more fantastic than is the other, that it is a Third Century polemic of political realism. It has the merit, at least, of being in harmony with the universal Taoist belief and of defending the name of Laotzu.

The foregoing suggestion explains the many singular likenesses in its thoughts and even words to the teachings of Buddhism, and it further explains why in the following centuries as Indian Buddhism came into China that it found an affinity with the Laotzuan philosophy and was profoundly influenced by it, until by the Sixth Century A. D. the type of

Buddhism taught by Hui-neng, the Sixth Patriarch of Dhyana Buddhism, became indigenous. Substantially all the very early leaders of Buddhism in China were Taoist scholars and for a thousand years, even down to today, it is often hard to say whether Buddhism is more Buddhistic or Taoist. Buddhist temples and Taoist Temples, in both images and ceremonial, are often almost indistinguishable. This very translation was made in a Brotherhood that first bow in adoration to Maitreya Buddha and then turn to bow to Taoist worthies and to the name of Laotzu. The Pure Land type of Buddhists first started in just this way of synthesizing the conceptions of Tao and Buddhahood but later veered over to a more exclusive adoration of the name of Amitabha Buddha, and, by so doing, departed from the free and un-theistic spirit of Shakyamuni, which is preserved in the conception of Tao. I have written more at length of this origin of Dhyana Buddhism in China in an essay that is included in my book entitled, A Buddhist Bible; the Favorite Scriptures of the Zen Sect, and therein show at some length the steps of this influence of the *Tao-teh-king* upon early Buddhism as it developed in China.

DWIGHT GODDARD.

THE CENTRAL TEACHING OF LAOTZU

In Chow Cheh in King Shao District of Hopeh Province (formerly Chili) on Tsung Nan mountain is a Taoist Temple known as Tsung Sun Kung. This temple is said to have been built to mark the place where Laotzu wrote the Tao-teh-king. At this place was a frontier post and to this post five hundred years before the Christian Era came an old man going to the far West. The guard recognized him as a sage and after talking with him, asked him to write down his teaching. This the old philosopher did in this small book of five thousand characters which ever since has been recognized the world over as one of the great classics.

It has been translated into many languages, but owing to its very condensed style, the translations often miss the full meaning of the obscure characters. Indeed, to fully grasp its teaching every word must be understood. There are hundreds of commentaries written upon it during the more than two thousand years that have past since it was written. The present translation has been made after studying many of these commentaries and talking with different Taoist masters and hermits.

The central teaching is the conception of TAO. It would hardly be right to make use of the teaching of Buddhism, perhaps, to elucidate the meaning of this Tao conception, yet the profound and mysterious Tao, in its essence, is really another word for the Buddhist conception of Tathata. Both stand for the ultimate "suchness" that is what it is. If they differ, Tao refers more directly to the principle of the self-nature of Ultimate reality while Tathata refers more directly to the essence of it. But in Ultimate reality principle and essence are an inscrutable oneness.

Going along with this central teaching are two others. The first is *wu-wei*. The characters mean, not acting, or not interfering, or non-assertion. In its negative aspect it means resisting and controlling one's finite nature in the interest of its infinite Taohood. In its positive aspect it is realizing enlightenment and Taohood. Before one can attain Enlightenment and Buddhahood he must emancipate his mind from all discriminations of ideas, thoughts and desires either of evil and good, or both, or neither. This is what is meant by the attainment of wu-wei in its relation to Taohood. With the attainment of wu-wei the veil of the finite mind is opened revealing the Eternal Light. By practising *wu-wei* one is able to manifest all good qualities, such as kindness, sympathy, compassion, joy and equanimity, transcendental powers and highest perfect wisdom, for the benefit of all sentient beings.

The second is the conception of *Teh*. The character means spiritual power or virtue. It is not revealed intentionally, it flows out naturally and spontaneously. It does not interfere, it cooperates with sympathy, uninfluenced by any ulterior desires or ideas. "Evil is aggravated when righteous ideas of superior men are made up into social codes, which if not obeyed willingly are enforced by law. (No.). Essential virtue is characterized by the absence of self-assertion.

There are many exceedingly close similarities between the teachings of the *Tao-teh-king* and Buddhism. For instance:—In No. it is written, "As rivers have their source in some far off fountain, so the human spirit has its own source. To find this fountain of spirit is to learn the secret of heaven and earth. In this Fountain of Mystery, spirit is eternally present in endless supply. Anyone can avail himself of it for the refreshment and unfolding greatness of his own spirit, by the earnest practice of mental concentration, but to do so he must do so with wu-wei of mind and sensitive expectancy." This is precisely the Buddhist practice of Dhyana. In this connection see, also, No. . "If in our practice of concentration, our heavenly eye is suddenly opened and we gain enlightenment, etc." See also, Nos. , , and .

One of the most characteristic teachings of Buddhism is the control of the desires. No. is devoted to inculcating the control of the sensual desires, and in No. it is written,—"As soon as things are given names, greed and grasping arise and unless one knows when to stop, there will be no satisfying the desires. To know when to be satisfied and to restrain desire is to know the secret of longevity. This is the principle of Tao."

In Buddhism Wisdom and Compassion are potential within the Universal Mind and therein abide in emptiness and silence. In No. it is written,—"There is a primal essence that is all inclusive and undifferentiated and which existed before there was any appearance of heaven and earth. How tranquil and empty it is! How self-sufficing and changeless! How omnipresent and infinite! Yet this tranquil emptiness become the Mother of all." In No. ,—"Perfect homogeneity appears as emptiness but its potentiality is never exhausted." And in No. ,—"When the potentiality of Tao manifests itself, it becomes the mother of all things."

In Buddhism another characteristic teaching is its depreciation of intellectual knowledge and its appreciation of intuitive wisdom. In No. it is written,—"When people abandon the idea of becoming a sage and give up the ambition for worldly knowledge and learning, then their innate goodness will have a chance to manifest itself and will develop a hundred fold."

If it was conceivable that the teachings of Shakyamuni could have percolated into China as early as the Fourth Century B.C., one would feel warranted in believing that Laotzu must have known them. As it is, it is an instance of two great minds living at substantially the same time, thinking the same thoughts. Both saw the solution of human evils and suffering by a return to the purity and simplicity of their eternal source (No.) . May the people of England and America as they come to understand the full significance of Laotzu's conception of Tao find it a golden key that will open the inestimable treasures within the mystery of their own minds.

BHIKKSHU WAI-TAO.

LAOTZU' S TAO-TEH-KING

A new translation from the Chinese by
WAI-TAO and DWIGHT GODDARD

PART ONE: TAO

ONE

The TAO that can be "tao-ed" can not be the infinite TAO (that is, the way that can be followed can not be the ultimate, pathless Way) . It is the same with the name of things: if things are explicable, the names we give them can not be the original Name. (That is) The course of the universe is hidden in non-existence; existence is only the mother of its evolution.

Since human beings are a small likeness of the great Universe, they can only realize their Taohood by making close imitations of it. Before one can attain the supreme perfection of Taohood, he must first realize its inmost mystery, that is, he must enter the door of this mystery of mysteries.

There are two ways for effecting this realization, both of which can be followed by the human organism. One way to realize the wonderful mystery of TAO is to put away all thoughts and desires. The other way is to concentrate both true intention and sincere devotion. These two ways of realization have different names but they both lead to a realization of the mystery that we call TAO.

TWO

Our minds naturally perceive the beauty of things on account of their beautifulness; so they also have a feeling of disgust for their ugliness on account of their ugliness. It is the same with goodness and badness. Everything in the world is mutually opposing and revealing itself.

So existence and non-existence are mutually related; the difficult and the easy are always in combination; the long and the short always qualify each other; the high and the low are always in opposition; the loud and the soft are loud and soft only in contrast with each other; the before and the behind are contrasted but always keep company.

Therefore the perfect Sage in avoiding the limitations of relativity resorts to no compulsion, nor does he make invidious comparisons in teaching his people. Whatever he does is done in harmony with the principle of TAO. Whatever he produces is not kept in his own possession; whatever he does is not exhibited with pride; whatever he accomplishes is not dwelt upon with self-conceit. Because he avoids possession, and pride and self-conceit, his accomplishments are kept in lasting memory.

THREE

If the perfect Sage would have his people give up their rivalries, he should not praise the competent ones. If he would have his people keep away from robbery and theft, he should not value precious things himself. If he would keep his mind undisturbed he should not look at desirable things. Thus the administration of the perfect Sage is designed to remove the desires of his people. He supplies them only with suitable nourishment and lessens their individual ideas by strengthening the common physical health. He ever tries to keep his people in ignorance and desirelessness so as to prevent the brainy ones from undertaking trouble-making activities. So long as he governs his people by the principle of *wu-wei* (non-assertion, or non-compulsion), things naturally arrange themselves into social order.

FOUR

TAO is invisible but permeates everywhere; no matter how one uses it or how much, it is never exhausted. It is wise for us to imitate its profoundness; that is, to keep ourselves in quiet confidence as being the unfailing source of all things. We should hide our wits and competencies; we should free ourselves from worldly entanglements; keep ourselves always in humility and courtesy; becoming ever more socialized and personally disinterested.

Should we attain all of these conditions, we would become as still and as transparent as the pure water of a spring. Then we would not recognize any spiritual forefather because no one would be worthy to be our ancestor except the perfect Father, the Great TAO.

FIVE

Heaven and earth are not fallible and unjust like humans: they are always impartial. They have no favorites in giving kindness to the world: they give life to humans with the same impartiality they give life to dogs and plants. The perfect sage is also impartial: he has no prejudices that would lead him to like this one and dislike that one; he treats all men as being of equal value. Moreover, there is nothing between heaven and earth but vast space. Heaven and earth resemble a bellows and a musical pipe: they are empty but inexhaustible; the more one plays on them the more they give out. The babbler is constantly being confounded but the dumb sage, constantly exercising concentration of mind, is competent to meet every chance and circumstance.

SIX

As rivers have their source in some far off fountain, so the human spirit has its source. To find his fountain of spirit is to learn the secret of heaven and earth. In this fountain of mystery, spirit is eternally present in endless supply. Anyone can avail himself of it for the refreshment and the unfolding greatness of his own spirit by the earnest practice of concentration, but to do so he must devote himself to the effort with *wu-wei* of mind and sensitive expectancy.

SEVEN

Heaven is eternal and earth is everlasting. The reason why heaven and earth are eternal is because they do not live for or by themselves: that is the reason they ever endure.

The perfect Sage, who puts his own interests behind him, is always the leader of his people. All the time he is looking after the welfare of his people and in doing so he preserves his own life. Is it not because he is disinterested that his own interests are conserved?

EIGHT

The highest virtue is like water: it benefits everything without exciting rivalries. We should be like water, choosing the lowest place which all others avoid. We are then closely akin to TAO.

For our dwelling we should choose the place where we can be of most benefit to our neighbors; we should be kind and courteous, always choosing to be with good people; in speech we should only speak words of truth and kindness; in administration we should seek to keep things in peace and order; in affairs we should exercise our best abilities; in activities we should adjust ourselves as circumstances arise and change.

Inasmuch as we are never seeking pre-eminence, no one will hate us.

NINE

To stop one's desires is far better than to be continually satisfying them. Desire is like a knife: if it is continually being sharpened, it will soon wear away.

There are wealthy men with mansions filled with gold and jewels, but they must be on the watch all the time to protect them. The pride of wealth and position brings about its own destruction. As soon as one has gained merit and fame, he should withdraw into retirement. This is the TAO of Heaven.

TEN

During the daytime, our senses are kept busy in activities, but if we keep our minds concentrated, we will better preserve their potentialities. If, in our practice of concentration, we preserve humility and tenderness and retain our natural breathing, we will become like a little child. If, in our practice of concentration, our minds retain their purity, we will be kept free from faults.

If the perfect Sage truly loves his people and wishes to bring his state into peace and order, he must practice *wu-wei*. If in our practice of concentration our heavenly eye is suddenly opened and we gain enlightenment thenceforth we shall be free from lust and greed. If we attain transcendental intelligence, our minds penetrating into every corner and into everything, then our minds will lose their self-consciousness.

A father begets children and sustains them while they are growing, nevertheless his children are not to be considered as his personal property, nor is his care of them to be done for any hope of reward, nor should his parental authority continue after they have reached manhood. This is the profoundest virtue of TAO.

ELEVEN

There are thirty spokes in a wheel, but its utility lies in the hole of the hub. The potter forms the clay into jars, but their usefulness depends upon the enclosed space. A carpenter builds the walls of a house and cuts out windows and doors, but the value of the house is measured by the space within the walls. Thus it may be said that existence is for accommodation but non-existence is for utility.

TWELVE

If a man indulges his desire for looking at the five beautiful colors, his perception of their beauty will become dull; if a man indulges a desire for listening to the five musical tones, his perception of their music will become dulled; if he indulges a desire for the five pleasant tastes, his perception of their deliciousness will become dull. If a man indulges a desire for racing and hunting, he will lose his appreciation of tranquillity and may become mad. So it is with the lure of hidden treasure that tempts a man to do evil.

Therefore the perfect Sage aims at usefulness and is not deceived by the illusions of sense. A man in hunger desires food to satisfy his hunger and is little concerned by its beauty and delicacy.

THIRTEEN

Favor and disgrace are both to be feared; too great care of the body and too great neglect of the body are both to be feared. To be favored is humiliating, so to attain it is as much to be dreaded as to lose it. That is what is meant by favor and disgrace are alike to be feared.

Why do our greatest troubles lie in too great care of our body? It is because one by so doing is all the time remembering that he has a body. As soon as I forget that I have a body then the troubles of the body vanish.

Therefore, if a man is willing to give up his body for the benefit of the state, he is worthy to be entrusted with the state. It is the same with the perfect Sage who forgets his body in the service of the people; he is best qualified to govern the empire.

30

FOURTEEN

There is one thing in the universe that we can not see with our eyes, nor hear with our ears, nor grasp by our perceiving mind, but that which our senses fail to perceive or our mind fails to grasp yet may be realized in meditation. When we look upward we can not see its brightness, when we look downward we can not perceive its existence. Although this mystery is always present there is no adequate name for it.

If we concentrate our mind upon it, our mind becomes unified with it and becomes as empty as open space. This is what may be called the form of the formless, the image of the imageless. It is as if we were in a trance. When we meet it we can not see its face and when we follow it we can not see its back. If, in dhyana, we tranquilize our minds by the *wu-wei* principle of TAO, some day we will realize our identity with its mystery. Then we are true apostles of TAO.

FIFTEEN

In olden times those who were competent to be Masters were intelligent, subtle, profound and spiritual. Their thoughts could not be easily fathomed. Since their thoughts were hard to comprehend, I will try to reveal their virtue by some explanation. They were as cautious as a man crossing a river in winter; they were as suspicious as a man who fears his neighbors; they were as circumspect as a guest in the presence of his host; they were as ready to adapt themselves as ice at the point of melting; they were as true and sound as the trunk of a perfect tree; they were as open and broadminded as a spacious valley; their thoughts were obscure like troubled waters.

Who can enlighten himself by slowly quieting the troubled waters of his mind? After gaining calmness of mind by concentration, who can gradually pass from its calmness into the activities of life and always retain the same calmness of mind? Only those who keep themselves from self-sufficiency and who control their lives by the principle of TAO. Being free from self-sufficiency, their spirit and energy will never fail, but will ever be refreshed and renewed.

SIXTEEN

At the moment when one is able to concentrate his mind to the extreme of emptiness and is able to hold it there in serene tranquillity, then his spirit is unified with the spirit of the universe and it has returned to its original state from which his mind and all things in the universe have emerged as appearance.

All things are in a recurring process of appearing and disappearing only to return to their original state. This may be called a kind of inertia, a drag on activity and manifestation, that brings all things back to their original state of composure. The original state is eternal. To understand this eternality of emptiness is enlightenment; without this enlightenment one's mind is engrossed in confusion and evil activity.

Understanding this truth of eternality makes one merciful; mercy leads one to be impartial; impartiality results in nobility of character; nobility is like heaven. To be heavenly means to have attained Taohood. To have attained Taohood is to become unified with eternity. One can never die even with the decay of his body.

SEVENTEEN

A great ruler, first of all, ought to know the necessities and habits of his people. Secondly, he should keep in close touch with them and praise the meritorious ones. Thirdly, he should give reason for them to respect his moral earnestness. Lastly, he should resort to punishment only to bring home to them the disgracefulness of evil.

When a ruler lacks faith in his people, his people will lack faith in him. A wise ruler is always careful in his choice of words and because of it his people respect him and give him credit for the natural success of his admiration.

EIGHTEEN

When people no longer follow the great TAO, they originate the ideas of benevolence and righteousness. When knowledge and learning are cultivated there is hypocrisy. When relatives are unfriendly to one another, they adopt the teaching of filial piety and paternal affection. When a country is in confusion and discord, ideals of loyalty and patriotism arise.

NINETEEN

When people abandon the idea of becoming a sage and give up ambition for worldly knowledge and learning, then their innate goodness will have a chance to manifest itself and will develop a hundredfold. When there is no activity of thinking to interfere, there is nothing that the mind can not accomplish in the way of good self-development. If ideas of benevolence and righteousness are abandoned, then people will return naturally to the primal virtues of filial piety and parental affection. If craftiness and acquisitiveness are abandoned, then theft and robbery will naturally disappear.

The reason why I refer to this is because of the deficiency of these primal virtues in our present culture. Let us restrain our sensual desires and egoism and return to simplicity and naturalness.

TWENTY

Abandon your acquired learning and do not regret the loss. There is very little difference between 'yes' and 'no', but what a vast difference between a good man and a wicked man. There are some things (like suffering and death) which are universally feared and which it is natural to fear, but woe to those ignorant people who desire and grasp after amusements and defilements (the very things that cause suffering and death) . People are busy with enjoyments as if they were celebrating a feast day, or as if they were flocking to the games. I, alone, am as fresh as the morning air, as pure as a babe in its mother's arms, as free as a homeless wanderer. Other people are admired and envied because of their cleverness; I, alone, am neglected. Am I (because of this) foolish at heart? No! Let them be as smart and aggressive as ever; I am content to remain retiring and obscure. Let them continue to be as sensible and prudent as ever; let me remain as neglected as a deaf-mute.

Nevertheless, I am as pure as the water in the ocean and as free as the driftwood upon its bosom. Let others have their means for acquiring wealth, I am content to be counted foolish and inefficient. I seem to stand in contrast to common people, empty and foolish, but I am nourished by food from Mother TAO.

TWENTY-ONE

All the innumerable forms of *teh* (power or virtue) correspond to the principle of TAO, but the nature of TAO is to be realized only in a state of mental concentration when the thinking mind is empty and quiescent and the intuitive mind is alert and receptive. Then the spirit reflects reality and realizes its true nature. When the spirit is in an advanced state of tranquillity, there will, be opened a fountain of purest semen available for service which by its special signs can be recognized intuitively. Since the beginning, this generative vitality has ever been available for the creation and nourishment of all things. Moreover, the reason one can comprehend the mystery of Originality is simply because of the fertilization by his same vitality called TAO.

TWENTY-TWO

Time will show that the humblest will attain supremacy, the dishonored will be justified, the empty will be filled, the old will be rejuvenated, those content with little will be rewarded with much, and those grasping much will fall into confusion.

Therefore, the perfect Sage who keeps his mind unified and humble will become the master of the world. As he has no prejudices, he becomes enlightened; as he does not assert himself, he will become exalted; as he does not praise himself, his merit will be recognized; as he is not proud of himself, his fame will endure; inasmuch as he does not seek supremacy, he will have no rivals.

True, indeed, is the old saying: "The humble will be exalted." Every one, with sincerity, should take refuge in humility.

TWENTY-THREE

To have an empty and transparent mind and to be unassertive is according to nature. A whirlwind never outlasts the morning, nor a violent rain the day. What causes the whirlwind and a violent rain? Is it not because of special condition of heaven and earth? If even nature can not keep up its disturbances for very long, how can a man expect to long assert himself?

Therefore, he who is devoting his life to the attainment of TAO, should be sincerely humble in mind and unassertive in his activities. If he is with those who are following TAO, he should show sympathy by following TAO himself. If he is with those who are practising *teh*, he should practise *teh*, also. If he is with those who have suffered loss, he should show sympathy with them in their loss.

For he who shows sympathy with those who are following TAO will thereby attain his own Taohood; he who shows sympathy with those who are practising *teh*, will rejoice in the acquirement of more *teh* himself, he who shows sympathy with those in loss will know better how to bear his own loss.

If one lacks faith in himself, it is because he lacks faith in TAO.

TWENTY-FOUR

He that stands on tiptoe can not long stand steady; he that is sitting astride can not walk; he that is prejudiced can not become enlightened; he that is self-assertive can not become distinguished; he that praises himself will not be given credit by others; he that takes pride in himself will not long be able to retain his safety and fame.

The comparison of these illustrations to TAO is like comparing offal to food, or like comparing superficial manners with true sympathy of heart. Even animals recognize the difference and show hatred. Therefore, one who has attained Taohood will never manifest these egoistic qualities. He will avoid thinking of himself and will remain humble at heart.

TWENTY-FIVE

There is a primal essence that is all-inclusive and undifferentiated and which existed before there was any appearance of heaven and earth. How tranquil and empty it is! How self-sufficing and changeless! How omnipresent and infinite! Yet this tranquil emptiness becomes the Mother of all. Who knows its name? I can only characterize it and call it TAO. Though it is quite inadequate, I will even call it the Great. But how boundless is its Greatness! It stretches away into the far distances (like a circle) only to return again.

How Great is TAO! But so is Heaven Great; and so is earth Great; and so is the perfect Sage Great. On the earth there are these four Greatnesses and among them is the perfect Sage. Men act in conformity with the laws of earth; earth acts in conformity with the laws of Heaven; Heaven acts in conformity with the laws of TAO; TAO acts in accordance with its own self-nature.

TWENTY-SIX

As the heavy is the foundation of the light, so the quiet is master of the passionate. Therefore, the perfect Sage in all the experiences of the day does not lose his serenity. Though he be surrounded by grandeur, he will keep himself unconcerned and simple.

But, alas, for those emperors, masters of ten thousand chariots, who, recklessly ambitious for power, have grasped after riches and thereby have lost control of their empires. If a king be reckless and flippant, he will lose the respect of his subjects; if he give way to passion, he will lose control of his kingdom.

TWENTY-SEVEN

Good walkers need no guides; good speakers do not blame or reproach others; good managers need no rules nor diagrams; good locksmiths are competent to open any lock; good binders can unloose any kind of knot.

It is the same with the perfect Sage: he is always competent in giving advice to his people, so that not one becomes an outcast. He is competent in using things, so that nothing is useless to him. His insight detects hidden values. Therefore the competent man is the master of the incompetent, and the incompetent are as hands and feet to the competent. The incompetent who does not esteem his master and the competent who does not protect his hands and feet, though he otherwise be intelligent, is acting foolishly. Herein lies the value of intelligence.

TWENTY-EIGHT

He who realizes the foolishness of passionate action always keeps his mind concentrated and tranquil. Just as the valleys, because of their lowness, become the source of rivers, so the perfect Sage because of his characteristic humility returns to the simplicity of a little child.

He who realizes the true way of conserving his spirit will take good care of his body. Thereby he becomes an example to the world. His original vitality will never fail, and more, will return to its origin.

He who realizes the dignity of his personality, but retains his humility, is like the lowly valley. Being like a valley, he becomes filled with the original vitality and reverts to his original nature. But when he forsakes humility, he merely becomes cultivated and useful. The perfect Sage employs these cultivated and useful men to become his officials and chiefs. Therefore a good administrator makes no reforms that will destroy the natural simplicity of his people.

TWENTY-NINE

If anyone desires to take and remake the empire under his own reforming plans, he will never be successful. The empire is a spiritual thing that cannot be remade after one's own ideas and he who attempts it will only make a failure. Even he who tries to hold it will lose it.

Under any system of holding or remaking the empire, the king must make use of different people and things; some of whom are honorable and precious and others are of less degree; some will be leaders and some will be only ornamental; some will be followers and some servants. Some people or things are strong and can be depended upon, others are fragile and will break or must be thrown away.

Therefore, the perfect Sage does not seek to take and remake the empire. He does not seek to enforce his own ideas upon it, but is content to give up extravagant comforts and indulgent egoism himself and thus to set the nation an example of returning to simplicity.

THIRTY

When a minister serves a ruler after the principle of TAO, he will not advise a resort to force of arms to become a great nation. Like returns to like. So briars and thorns grow rank where an army camps. Bad years of want and disorder follow a great war.

Therefore, the competent ruler, resolutely restraining his desires and ambition, dares not resort to force. Because he is resolute, he will not be boastful, nor haughty, nor arrogant; because he is resolute he will act only under necessity; because he is resolute, he will have no ambition to be powerful.

By the nature of things, when the strength of anything is fully developed, it immediately begins to decay. This means that strength is not in accordance with the principle of TAO. Being not in accordance with TAO, it will soon pass away.

THIRTY-ONE

Both arms and armor are unblessed things. Not only men come to detest them, but a curse seems to follow them. Therefore, the one who follows the principle of TAO does not resort to arms. It is significant that in peaceful times, the place of honor is on the left and in war times it is on the right. For as arms are unblessed things, they are not the things that men of good character resort to.

It is of first importance for a gentleman to preserve his serenity and dignity; even when victorious, a good soldier does not rejoice, because rejoicing over a victorious battle is the same as rejoicing over the killing of men. If he rejoices over the killing of men, he will never be victorious.

Thus, in propitious affairs, the place of honor is on the left, but in unpropitious affairs, the right is the place of honor. In times of war, lesser officers are on the left of the ranks, a place of honor, while the commanding general is on the right, a place of less honor. This means that war is considered as a funeral ceremony.

Therefore, in battle the killing of many men should be honored by weeping and mourning, and the victor should be received as if he were attending a funeral ceremony.

THIRTY-TWO

TAO is eternal but is unnamable. Its simplicity, though considered as of the humblest, is most independent. Nothing in the world is able to bring it into subjection. If princes and kings retain simplicity heaven and earth are harmoniously unified and, everywhere drop the sweet dew of their favor naturally and evenly.

As soon as things are given names, greed and grasping arise and, unless one understands when to stop, there will be no satisfying the desires. To know when to be satisfied and to restrain desire, is to know the secret of longevity. This is the principal of TAO. It resembles the great rivers that flow into the seas, but which have their origin in the little streams of the valleys.

THIRTY-THREE

He who understands others is intelligent; he who understands himself is enlightened. He who is able to conquer others is powerful; he who can control himself is more powerful.

He who is contented is richer than the richest. Those who have purpose are resolute, and those who keep tranquillity of mind have endurance. Those whose fame endures beyond death are immortal.

THIRTY-FOUR

Great TAO is all pervading! It is available everywhere, on the right hand and on the left. Everything is dependent upon it for existence and it never fails them. It does all this but claims no ownership. As TAO has no selfish desires and is perfectly humble, everything takes refuge in it. Because it does not care for ownership, it is regarded as the greatest. Because the perfect Sage never thinks of his greatness, he can attain true Greatness.

THIRTY-FIVE

The whole world is naturally drawn to him who keeps this principle of TAO'S true Greatness. It goes to TAO and receives no harm; on the contrary it finds contentment, tranquillity and peace. To common people TAO'S principle of simplicity and humility seems weak and insipid; they desire and seek music and dainties. Indeed, TAO has no taste! When looked at, there is nothing to be prized; when listened for, it can scarcely be heard; but its satisfactions are inexhaustible.

THIRTY-SIX

Before one can contract a thing, it must first be extended; before anything can be weakened, it must first be made strong; before anything can be wasted, it must be present; before one can take a thing by force, someone else must give it up. This is the profound principle which explains why the humble and yielding conquer the selfish and strong.

A fish should not be removed from its natural home in the deep pond, neither should the authority of the nation be entrusted to anyone, not even to the king's favorite.

THIRTY-SEVEN

TAO acts without assertion, yet all things proceed in conformity with it. If princes and kings would follow the principle of TAO, then all things would unfold according to their own nature. If there are troublesome desires arising from the habits of the people, they should be taught the principle of simplicity that characterizes the ineffable TAO.

Even the conception of the ineffable TAO's simplicity ought not to remain in one's mind. When quietness is attained, not by ideas and the satisfaction of desires but by the practice of non-assertion, the troubles of the world will right themselves.

PART TWO: TEH

THIRTY-EIGHT

The *teh* (power, or virtue) of the perfect Sage is not revealed intentionally. It naturally and spontaneously meets the needs of the world and, therefore, it is the true teh of TAO. The teh of inferiors simply makes an outside show of power which is assumed to be virtue, therefore, it falls short of the true Teh.

The Teh of the perfect Sage does not interfere, it cooperates with open and sympathetic mind, while the teh of inferiors acts with intention and under conditions and is influenced by desires. The benevolence of the perfect Sage flows out naturally in acts of kindness and is unconditioned by desires, or ideas, or conditions; while righteousness, even of superior men, is done under conditioning desires and ideas. This evil is aggravated when these righteous ideas of superior men are made up into social codes, which if not obeyed willingly are enforced by law.

Therefore, when one loses TAO, he makes use of teh as a standard of living; when he loses teh, he makes use of benevolence as a standard; when one loses benevolence, he makes use of righteousness; when he loses righteousness he makes use of social codes as his standard of conduct. Thus social codes take the place of loyalty and faith and there is the beginning of disorder. Cultural civilizations are a mere shadow of TAO and are the source of allurements and foolishness.

Therefore, the superior man of affairs conforms to the spirit of Teh and not to its reduction into codes of loyalty and righteousness. He abides in the reality of TAO and not in its shadow.

THIRTY-NINE

From the beginning there has been a law of unity. Heaven attained unity and thereby its perfect clearness; earth attained unity and thereby its solidity; spirit attained unity and thereby its subtilty; valleys attained unity and thereby became the source of rivers; everything in the world attained unity and thereby their power of growth; princes and kings attained unity and thereby attained to moral conduct. Everything unfolds by the same law into some form of unity.

For if heaven were not purity it would differentiate; if earth were not solidity it would crumble and fall apart; if spirit were not subtilty it would lose its vitality; if valleys were not ever flowing out, they would soon fill up; if things were not growing, they would soon come to destruction; when princes and kings decline in moral conduct, they soon lose the respect of their subjects and forfeit their kingdoms.

Unless nobles serve the interests of the common people, they are no longer noble; the high need the low for a foundation. The reason why princes and kings refer to themselves as "the forlorn," "the inferior," and "the unworthy," is because they understand the principle that nobles require common people as a basis for their nobility.

When a carriage is separated into its parts it is no longer a carriage, its unity is lost. The superior man should not desire to become cultivated and shine as a gem, neither should he become gross and dull as stones. There should be a unity of ideals and usefulness.

FORTY

To withdraw the mind from attention to outward things, to be thoughtful, to practice meditation, is to be in conformity with TAO. To be humble and of service to others is, also, being in conformity with TAO. Heaven and earth, and all things are manifestations of existence, but existence, itself, comes from non-existence. (It is to this potential nonexistence that the mind should be directed) .

FORTY-ONE

The superior man, as soon as he listens to TAO, earnestly practices TAO; an average man, hearing of TAO, sometimes remembers it and sometimes forgets it; an inferior man, hearing of TAO, ridicules it. If it were not thus ridiculed it would not be worth following as TAO.

There is an old saying:—"Those who are illuminated by TAO are the most obscure; those who are advanced in TAO are the most timid; those who are indifferent to TAO are the most distinguished." The Teh of TAO resembles a deep valley; the most innocent appears to be most ashamed; the highest in teh appears the humblest; the most firmly established in teh appears the most remiss; the most straightforward seems to be the most fickle; the greatest polygon has no corners; the finest instrument is the latest to be perfected; the largest bell sounds rarely; the grandest phenomena are the inconceivable phenomena of spirit.

TAO is unseen and inscrutable. Nevertheless, it is precisely this TAO that alone can give and accomplish.

FORTY-TWO

TAO is inscrutable. From TAO proceeds the one (potentiality); one produces two (the positive and negative principles); this makes three. From these three proceed all things. All things thus bear the imprint of the negative *yin* behind and embrace the positive *yang* in front. The primal principle of potentiality, as it becomes active, brings the negative and positive together and there is manifestation.

The things that are detested by common people, namely, to be called the forlorn, the inferior, the unworthy, are the very things that kings and princes take for titles. These are the very things that it is a gain to lose and a loss to gain.

I am teaching the same thing which is taught by others; others have said that the strong and aggressive do not come to natural deaths, but I make this saying the basis of my teaching.

FORTY-THREE

The tenderest things of creation prevail over the hardest. Something immaterial enters into the most impenetrable to preserve its unity. I, therefore, recognise the advantages of the principle of *wu-wei* and teach non-interference. There is no other doctrine that is grander than the doctrine of TAO, and no other teaching that is more universally potent than the teaching of *wu-wei*.

FORTY-FOUR

Which is more intimately precious: fame or life? Which is more valuable: life or treasure? Which gives the most trouble: gain or loss? One naturally seeks the things he most prizes; for that reason we should be careful to prize the right things, because grasping and hoarding invite waste and loss both to property and life.

A contented person is never dishonored. One who knows how to stop with enough is free from danger; he will therefore endure.

FORTY-FIVE

The enlightenment of the perfect Sage, because of its simplicity, appears as lacking, but his wisdom never fails. Perfect homogeneity appears as emptiness, but its potentiality is never exhausted. Extreme frankness appears as evasive, great skill as clumsiness, great eloquence as stammering. Motion conquers cold, while quietness conquers heat. Purity and tranquillity are the true characteristics of creation.

FORTY-SIX

When the world yields to the principle of TAO, its race horses will be used to haul manure; when the world ignores TAO, war horses are pastured on the public common.

There is no sin greater than yielding to desire. There is no misfortune greater than yielding to discontent. There is no greater folly than to yield to acquisitiveness. Thus, everyone should be contented for he that is contented is already rich.

FORTY-SEVEN

Not going out of the door, the sage has knowledge of the world. Not looking through the window, he perceives the TAO of heaven. The more one wanders about among objective things, the less he understands.

Therefore, the perfect Sage does not think about worldly affairs, but he understands the significance of all things. He does not boast of his ability, but his name is world famous. He' works but without grasping and, therefore succeeds in whatever he undertakes.

FORTY-EIGHT

In regard to knowledge: the more one studies, the more he accumulates learning; while in regard to wisdom the more one practices TAO, the more his desires and thoughts are lessened, even to perfect emptiness of mind, all his innate excellencies will be developed and manifested. It is therefore necessary, if one is to keep control of his mind, to preserve its emptiness. But as soon as one desires to control his mind, he becomes incapable of doing so. It is by this spontaneous control of mind that the Sage gains the world's favor.

FORTY-NINE

The perfect Sage has no preconceived opinions; he accepts the opinions of his people as his own. The good he treats with fairness, the not-good he also treats with fairness and by so doing attains the teh of justice. The faithful he treats with good-faith, and the unfaithful he also treats with good-faith and so he attains the teh of faithfulness.

The perfect Sage is always concerned about the welfare of people and, indeed, it is for their sakes that his mind is burdened. All people show him respect and are obedient to him and, in return, he regards them as his children.

FIFTY

The moon from its first appearance to full moon, is in a state of appearing; from its fullness to its disappearance, it is in a state of disappearing. It is just the same with the life of a man:. from babyhood to manhood he is growing up; from manhood to old age, he is failing. What does this signify? It means that it is only the spirit of man that shares the longevity of heaven and earth and, of all things heaven and earth are endowed with perennial vitality.

Thus it may be said that those who have attained mastery over their spirit, and thus have set free this perennial vitality, when traveling will never suffer harm from rhinoceros or tiger, or in battle without weapons or armor, because the rhinoceros will find no place to horn him, nor the tiger for its claws, nor will soldiers wound him. Why is this so? Because his spirit transcends mortality.

FIFTY-ONE

Life comes from TAO; its nourishment comes from teh; its shape is formed by materiality; its accomplishments are owing to energy. Therefore among all men there are none who do not honor TAO and esteem teh. Honor for TAO and esteem for teh is never by compulsion, it is always spontaneous. Men understand naturally that life comes from TAO and that teh nourishes them, raises them, nurtures them, completes, matures, rears, and protects them.

TAO gives life to them but does not exercise authority over them; teh forms them but makes no use of them, raises them but never interferes with them. This is the profound teh of the mysterious TAO.

FIFTY-TWO

When the potentiality of TAO manifests itself, it becomes the mother of all things. When one realizes that his life comes from this universal Mother, he will also realize his brotherhood to all her descendants. When one realizes his descent from the universal Mother and his brotherhood with all humanity, he will cherish his life and thus, to its end, will be kept in perfect health.

He who talks little and closes his sense gates will never become wearied to the end of life; he who talks much, and yields to the desires of his senses, and interferes with affairs, will be risking his life continually.

To be thoughtful and mindful is to be enlightened. To be humble and yielding is better than great strength. To use one's intelligence to seek enlightenment and to control one's body is to return to the nature of one's origin.

FIFTY-THREE

Should only one day be given me to carry out my wishes in explaining the principle of the Great TAO, I would condemn almsgiving as being a poisonous medicine, making people dependent. The Way of the Great TAO is wide and straight for men to follow, but most people prefer the bypaths.

When the royal palace is magnificent, fields become devastated and granaries empty. To wear ornaments and gay colors, to carry sharp swords, to indulge in dainties and excessive drinking, to hoard wealth and treasure, is simply to invite robbery. It is not the Way of the Great TAO.

FIFTY-FOUR

As a thing that is well planted is not easily uprooted and as a thing that is well guarded is not easily stolen, so if a family observes the principle of TAO, its descendants will ever hold their ancestors in honor.

He who practices TAO for himself will only gain teh for himself. He who practices TAO for the benefit of his family, his teh will pass to his descendants. If he practices TAO for the welfare of his community, his teh will be multiplied. If he practices TAO for the benefit of his country, his teh will become abundantly multiplied. If he practices the principle of TAO for the sake of the whole world, teh will become universal.

Therefore, he who practices TAO for himself will only himself be benefited. He who practices it for the sake of his family, will have his family benefited. He who practices it for his community will have his community benefited. He who practices TAO for the whole world will benefit the whole world.

How do I know all this? It comes from the practice of TAO.

FIFTY-FIVE

He who attains to the highest teh of simplicity and sincerity, may be compared to the ingenuousness of an infant. Poisonous insects do not sting their own young, wild beasts do not attack their own cubs, nor do birds of prey. A baby's bones may be weak and its muscles soft, but its spiritual vitality is perfect. An infant does not know about the relation of the sexes, but gradually its generative vigor will develop. Its spirit is virile, indeed! It may sob and cry all day but will not become hoarse. His unity as a child is perfect.

To understand how to preserve this unity and soundness, one must return to his original state of simplicity. To know how to return to one's original state is to be enlightened. To increase one's natural vigor means blessedness. To control one's breathing means strength. Things that are fully grown begin to decay, for growth is contrary to the principle of TAO. Things that are contrary to TAO soon pass away.

FIFTY-SIX

The wise keep silent; a babbler is not wise. Keep your mouth closed and guard the gates of sense. Hide your sharpness, free yourself from entanglements, conceal your personality, be socially minded and natural. Thus to harmonize one's life with the life of others is the teh of the profound TAO.

No one can befriend such a man, nor can they estrange him, nor endanger him, nor honor him, nor despise him. Such a man is naturally honored by all the world.

FIFTY-SEVEN

An empire is best administered by justice, an army by craft, and influence over people is gained by noninterference. The more people become selfish, the more the state is in disorder. The more people become artful and cunning, the more abnormal things become. The more laws and orders are multiplied, the more theft and violence increase.

Therefore, the perfect Sage reasons: If I practice *wu-wei*, that is, noninterference, the people will restrain themselves naturally. If I set an example of good behavior, people of themselves will become tranquil and prosperous naturally.

If I have no selfish desires myself, other people will become unselfish and simple.

FIFTY-EIGHT

If administrative restrictions be kept out of sight as much as possible, the people will become quiet, honest and sympathetic. If an administration becomes complex and officious, the people will become needy and turbulent.

Misery may be followed by happiness and happiness may lead to misery. Who can foretell the outcome of either misery or happiness? Is there no safe guide to normality? Indeed, normality itself soon becomes abnormal, and good conditions soon become unsatisfactory.

(Why is it necessary for justice to always become injustice, and for good conditions to always pass into evil?) It is because men have been under illusion for a long, long time. Therefore, the perfect Sage, though just himself, does not reprove another's injustice; though unselfish himself, he does not reprimand the covetousness of others; though he is straightforward, he does not offend others by disagreeable assertiveness; though wise, he does not make a show of his wisdom.

FIFTY-NINE

In governing people and in worshiping heaven, nothing surpasses the teh of self-restraint. The restraint of desire is like returning to the original TAO. Returning to one's origin means the recovery of one's vitality. When one has recovered his original vitality, nothing is unmanageable. If nothing is unmanageable then he retains his original tranquillity because he is unconscious of any limits. When he retains this state of tranquillity he may govern the country wisely. Moreover, when he is in a state of tranquillity, he will govern the country as a mother takes care of her children and by so doing long retain his usefulness. He will be like a plant having a strong stem and deep roots. He will manifest the longevity of TAO.

SIXTY

To govern a great state one should do it as a cook fries small fish, that is, without scaling or cleaning them.

If one rules an empire by the principle of TAO, spirits will lose their power. It is not because their power is any less, but because the people can no longer be harmed by them. Neither is it because of the harmlessness of the gods, but because of the harmlessness of the wise ruler. Since neither ghosts nor gods can harm people, if they have a wise ruler, they will return to that ruler good-will and they will abide in tranquillity.

SIXTY-ONE

A great state is like the current of a river; it is always flowing down the lower valleys. There is a bond of unity, also, in a great state that draws its people together, like the attraction of male to female.

The female wins the favor of a male by her quietude and quietude is always submissive. Thus a great state by its service to smaller states wins their allegiance. A smaller state by its submission to a great state wins an influence over it. Thus one wins by condescension, and the other by submission, and their interests are mutually conserved.

The great state likes to federate more states and have more people; the small state to guard its safety is willing to submit to the greater and enter its federation. Each by the same procedure gains its particular end. So it is a good policy for a great state to lead the way by itself first practicing humility.

SIXTY-TWO

TAO is an all-embracing mystery. It is treasure to good men and a refuge to bad men. Fine words are used in selling goods, but it is a noble life that wins the respect of others. Even though TAO is despised by common people, why should I be foolish as are they and ignore it?

In the establishment of a monarchy, (there are many things that are to be considered): the emperor is to be enthroned, the three ministers are to be appointed, the precious gems that have been presented to the emperor are to be distributed, and the tribute war-horses are to be properly exhibited. But nothing is more important than the dedication of the throne to TAO. For what reason did the ancients so highly esteem TAO? Was it not because it was only by devotion to TAO that the hopes of the nation could be realized and the miseries of the people relieved?

That is why TAO is honored by all the world.

SIXTY-THREE

A man's first duty is to practice *wu-wei* and make use of his quiet hours to gain enlightenment. One should early learn to find sweetness in tasteless things; to discover greatness in small things; to be satisfied with few things.

One should respond to hatred with kindness; he should treat little affairs as though they were important. All the world's difficulties arise from slight causes, and all the world's great affairs have risen from small beginnings.

Therefore, the perfect Sage never asserts his greatness and by so doing attains to true greatness. Rash promises are easily made, but the simpler a thing looks, the harder it is to accomplish. This is a common experience, therefore the perfect Sage considers everything difficult and so to the end has no difficulties.

SIXTY-FOUR

That which is at rest can easily be taken hold of. That which has not yet become important, can be easily prevented. The fragile is easily broken, light things are easily scattered. It is wise to be prepared for difficulties and to establish order before there is disorder. A tree that it takes both arms to encircle grew from a tiny rootlet. A many storied pagoda is built by placing one brick upon another brick. A journey of three thousand miles is begun by a single step. If one attempts to govern either himself or another, he is bound to make a failure of it. If he tries to grasp anything, it slips away from him.

The perfect Sage, therefore, by practicing *wu-wei* and making no attempts, makes no failures, and because he does not grasp anything, he has nothing to lose. People in their eagerness are ever approaching success only to continually fail. If one is to succeed, he must be as careful to the end as at the beginning.

Therefore, the perfect Sage has no desire for things that are difficult to obtain, nor does he value them. He learns to be unlearned; he turns away from that which others greedily seek. In that spirit he helps all things toward their natural development but dares not attempt to force their development.

SIXTY-FIVE

In the olden days, those who were well versed in the principle of TAO, avoided teaching the people anything; instead they kept them in ignorance. The reason why people are difficult to govern is because they are educated. To govern a people by craftiness is a curse; to govern them by the principle of *wu-wei* is a blessing. He who understands the difference between these two ways of governing is a model ruler. If he knows how to become a model ruler, he has gained profoundness of teh.

The profoundness of Teh is deep, indeed, and far reaching! Because it is in harmony with the original nature of things, everything will be acting according to the law of its nature.

SIXTY-SIX

The rivers and seas become the kings of the myriad valleys because they are content with the low places. The perfect Sage rises above his people because of his humility; because he is first willing to follow them, he comes to leadership.

Although the perfect Sage is above his people, yet they feel no burden; he dominates them, but they cherish no resentment. Therefore the world rejoices to exalt the perfect Sage and never wearies of him. Because he does not seek to rival others, others have no desire to rival him.

SIXTY-SEVEN

The world calls it the Great TAO, but there is nothing with which to compare it. Why? Simply because of its greatness. If there were anything with which to compare it, TAO would immediately become, and remain so for a long time, the most insignificant thing in all the world.

TAO has three treasures that are inherent in its very nature. The first is compassion; the second is economy; the third is humility. Because of his compassion, a man can become courageous. Because of his economy, a man may become generous. Because of his humility, a man can become a leader. Nowadays a man, because of discarding compassion, merely becomes bold; because of discarding economy, he only becomes extravagant; because of discarding humility, he becomes arrogant. Such men are already in the process of dying.

If a soldier is compassionate, in battle he will be a conqueror and in defense secure. If a man is compassionate, Heaven will protect him because of its compassion.

SIXTY-EIGHT

He who excels as a soldier is the man who is not warlike. He who fights the best fight is the man who does not lose his temper. He who truly conquers an enemy does not lord it over him but treats him with respect. He who best employs people keeps himself humble.

This is what is meant by the teh of non-rivalry. It is the way to bring out the good in others. It is the oldest principle that has ever been taught. It is in compliance with the nature of TAO.

SIXTY-NINE

It is taught in books of strategy: "Never be so rash as to start a war; at first, always be on the defense." "One should hesitate to advance an inch but be always ready to withdraw a foot." This means that it is better for an army to advance by craft rather than by aggressive operations. (It means for everybody) that there is a better way of attack than by hands, a better way of winning than by hostility, a better way of gaining than by resort to force. There is no greater mistake than to make light of an enemy. By-making light of an enemy many a kingdom has been lost. When well matched armies come to conflict, the army that regrets the hostility between them, always conquers.

SEVENTY

The principle of TAO is easy to understand and easy to put into practice, yet in all the world how few there are who understand it and put it into practice. Every word of common people has its object; every deed has its actor, but because these talkers and actors are ignorant, TAO is ignorant with them and does not interfere.

Since very few people know TAO, TAO is the more worthy of esteem. Therefore, the perfect Sage clothes himself in the cheap garments of poor people but keeps TAO, like a gem hidden in his bosom.

SEVENTY-ONE

To recognize one's ignorance of unknowable things is mental health and to be ignorant of knowable things is sickness. It is only by grieving over knowable things that we are kept in mental health. The perfect Sage is free from the mental sickness of common people, because he understands his ignorance and grieves over it.

SEVENTY-TWO

When people are too ignorant to fear the things that are really fearful (greed, illusion and self-assertion), the greatest fear (of death) will soon overpower them. Do not be troubled because of the narrowness of your dwelling, do not become depressed because of the life you are compelled to live. If people cease to worry about their surroundings and their lives, their minds will become tranquil.

Therefore, the perfect Sage understands himself but never exhibits himself; he cherishes but never overvalues himself. He discards ostentation and pride, but keeps understanding and mindfulness.

SEVENTY-THREE

Courage carried to recklessness leads to death, while courage restrained and cautious leads to life. Of these two kinds of courage, one is harmful and one is beneficial. Why this is so, why some things are rejected by Heaven and some not, who can tell the reason? Therefore the perfect

Sage looks upon all things as puzzling (and does not interfere with any).

The TAO of Heaven never seeks supremacy, yet it is always supreme. It speaks not but it is perfectly responsive. It issues no summons yet things come to it naturally. It appears to be open and simple, but hidden from view is a profound design. Indeed, the meshes of Heaven's net are wide, but no matter how wide or loose they may appear nothing escapes.

SEVENTY-FOUR

If people do not fear death, how can they be frightened by the death penalty? If people are afraid of death, I would seize the one who is not afraid of death and execute him. After that who would dare to disobey?

There is always an experienced officer to execute murderers. If an inexperienced person takes his place, it would be like an unskilled man taking the place of a skilled carpenter at his hewing: he is very likely to cut himself.

SEVENTY-FIVE

When a ruler appropriates too much of the taxes, starvation comes to the people. The reason why people are difficult to govern is because the ruler is thinking too much of his own interests. People make light of death because they are absorbed in the interests of life. The one who is not absorbed in life is wiser than he who esteems life.

SEVENTY-SIX

When a baby is born it is tender and fragile; when it grows to be a man and dies, it becomes hard and stiff. It is the same with everything.

Herbs and trees when young and growing are tender and delicate, but when they become old and die, they become rigid and hard.

Therefore, those who are stiff and unyielding belong to the domain of death, while the tender and sympathetic belong to the realm of life. Those who are ruthless in battle do not gain the victory. When a tree becomes hard and rigid, it will soon decay. The large and hard are put at the bottom, the tender and delicate are placed on top.

SEVENTY-SEVEN

The TAO of Heaven resembles the stretching of a bow. The mighty it humbles, the lowly it exalts; the overflowing it diminishes, the insufficient it supplies.

The way of humans is not so. Humans take from the needy to further enrich the rich. The one who can take from his over-abundance and give to a needy world has attained Taohood. Therefore, the perfect Sage is not sparing of his services, nor does he look upon them as meritorious, nor does he make a display of them. Is this not so?

SEVENTY-EIGHT

Nothing is more fragile than water, yet of all the agencies that attack hard substances nothing can surpass water, nor take its place. Therefore the weak are conquerors of the strong, and the yielding are conquerors of the mighty. Everyone knows this but few practice it.

Therefore, the perfect Sage accepts the disgrace of his country and by so doing becomes a true patriot; he is patient under the misfortunes of his country and because of it worthy to be its sovereign.

True words always seem paradoxical, but no other form of teaching can take its place.

SEVENTY-NINE

If nations hate each other but are making a treaty of peace, there will always remain some seeds of hatred. How can it be considered as a settlement?

The perfect Sage is always willing to accept the debit side of an account, for then he does not have to enforce payment from another. Those who have teh make unwritten contracts of faith; those who have no teh, make written contracts and hold them as evidence.

The TAO of Heaven makes no written contracts, but always helps the good man.

EIGHTY

In a small country with few people there will be in proportion many of exceptional merit and of competency but few vacancies for their services.

If people consider their death to be important, they will hesitate to go to distant countries. Though there be boats and carts they will have no occasion to use them. Though there be armor and weapons, there will be no occasion to don them. Let people return to the spirit of the olden days when they used knotted cords for their records; then they will take delight in simple food, be proud of their cheap clothes, content with their dwellings, and rejoice in their customs.

Neighboring states may be so close to each other that one can see them with their eyes, and their cocks and dogs can be mutually heard, but people will, have no desire to go and come even to the end of their lives.

EIGHTY-ONE

Faithful words are often not pleasant; pleasant words are often not faithful. Well informed men do not dispute; men who dispute are not well informed. The wise man is not always learned; the learned man is not always wise.

The perfect Sage does not keep things in possession or in memory, but since he ever serves others he acquires the most after all. Since he continually gives to others, he will possess the most in the end.

The TAO of Heaven always benefits and harms no one. The perfect Sage by following TAO and serving others is never the cause of strife.

ESSAYS INTERPRETING TAOISM

by
HENRI BOREL

Translated by
M. E. REYNOLDS

PREFACE

THE following study on Laotzu's "Wu-Wei" should by no means be regarded as a translation or even as a free rendering of the actual work of that philosopher. I have simply endeavoured to retain in my work the pure essence of his thought, and I have given a direct translation of his essential truths in isolated instances only, the rest being for the most part a self-thought-out elaboration of the few principles enunciated by him.

My conception of the terms "Tao" and "Wu-Wei" is entirely different from that of most sinologues (such as Stanislas Julien, Giles, and Legge), who have translated the work "Tao-Teh-King." But this is not the place to justify myself. It may best be judged from the following work whether my conception be reasonable or incorrect.

Little is contained in Laotzu's short, extremely simple book, the words of which may be said to be condensed into their purely primary significance—(a significance at times quite at variance with that given in other works to the same words *)—but this little is gospel. Laotzu's work is no treatise on philosophy, but contains, rather, merely those truths to which this (unwritten) philosophy had led him. In it we find no form nor embodiment, nothing but the quintessence of this philosophy.

My work is permeated with this essence, but it is no translation of Laotzu. None of my metaphorical comparisons, such as that with the landscape, with the sea, with the clouds, are anywhere to be found in Laotzu's work. Neither has he anywhere spoken of Art, nor specially of Love. In writing of all this I have spoken aloud the thoughts and feelings

---

*   By Confucius, for instance.

instinctively induced by the perusal of Laotzu's deep-felt philosophy. Thus it may be that my work contains far more of myself than I am conscious of; but even so, it is but an outpouring of the thought and feeling called up in me by the words of Laotzu.

I have made use of none but Chinese works on Laotzu, and of those only a few. On reading later some of the English and French translations, I was amazed to find how confused and unintelligible these books were.

I adhered to my simple idea of Laotzu's work, and of my work I could alter nothing, for I felt the truth of it within me as a simple and natural faith.

HENRI BOREL.

CHAPTER I

TAO

I WAS standing in the Temple of Shien Shan on an islet in the Chinese Sea, distant a few hours' journey from the harbour of Hâ Tó.

On either side rose mountain ranges, their soft outlines interwoven behind the island to the westward. To the eastward shimmered the endless Ocean. High up, rock-supported, stood the Temple, in the shadow of broad Buddha-trees.

The island is but little visited, but sometimes fisher-folk, fleeing before the threatening typhoon, anchor there when they have no further hope of reaching the harbour. Why the Temple exists in this lonely spot, no one knows; but the lapse of centuries has established its holy right to stand there. Strangers arrive but seldom, and there are only a hundred poor inhabitants, or thereabouts, who live there simply because their ancestors did so before them. I had gone thither in the hope of finding some man of a serious bent of mind with whom to study. I had explored the temples and convents of the neighborhood for more than a year, in search of earnest-minded priests capable of telling me what I was unable to learn from the superficial books on Chinese religion; but I found nothing but ignorant, stupid creatures everywhere—kneeling to idols whose symbolical significance they did not understand, and reciting strange "Sutras" not one word of which was intelligible to them. [1] And I had been obliged to draw all my information from badly translated works that had received even worse treatment at the hands of learned

Europeans than at those of the literary Chinese whom I had consulted. At last, however, I had heard an old Chinaman speak of "the Sage of Shien Shan" as of one well-versed in the secrets of Heaven and Earth; and—without cherishing any great expectations, it is true—I had crossed the water to seek him out.

This Temple resembled many others that I had seen. Grimy priests lounged on the steps in dirty-grey garments, and stared at me with senseless grins. The figures of "Kwan Yin" and "Cakyamuni" and "Sam-Pao-Fu" had been newly restored, and blazed with all imaginable crude colours that completely marred their former beauty. The floor was covered with dirt and dust, and pieces of orange-peel and sugar-cane were strewn about. A thick and heavy atmosphere oppressed my breast.

Addressing one of the priests, I said:

"I have come to visit the philosopher. Does not an old hermit dwell here, called after 'Laotzu'?"

With a wondering face he answered me:

"Laotzu lives in the top-most hut upon the cliffs. But he does not like barbarians."

I asked him quietly:

"Will you take me to him, Bikshu, for a dollar?"

There was greed in his glance, but he shook his head, saying:

"I dare not; seek him yourself."

The other priests grinned, and offered me tea, in the hope of a tip.—I left them, and climbed the rocks, reaching the top in half an hour; and there I found a little square stone hut. I knocked at the door, and, shortly after, heard some one draw back a bolt.

There stood the sage, looking at me.

And it was a revelation.

It seemed as though I saw a great light—a light not dazzling, but calming.

He stood before me tall and straight as a palm-tree. His countenance was peaceful as is a calm evening, in the hush of the trees, and the still

68

moonlight; his whole person breathed the majesty of nature, as simply beautiful, as purely spontaneous, as a mountain or a cloud. His presence radiated an atmosphere holy as the prayerful soul in the soft after-gleam on a twilight landscape,—I felt uneasy under his deep gaze, and saw my poor life revealed in all its pettiness. I could not speak a word, but felt in silence his enlightening influence.

He raised his hand with a gesture like the movement of a swaying flower, and held it out to me—heartily—frankly. He spoke, and his voice was soft music, like the sound of the wind in the trees:

"Welcome, stranger! What do you seek of me?—old man that I am!"

"I come to seek a master," I answered humbly, "to find the path to human goodness. I have long searched this beautiful land, but the people seem as though they were dead, and I am as poor as ever."

"You err somewhat in this matter," said the sage. "Strive not so busily to be so very good. Do not seek it overmuch, or you will never find the true wisdom. Do you not know how it was that the Yellow Emperor [2] recovered his magic pearl? I will tell you. [3]

"The Yellow Emperor once travelled round the north of the Red Sea, and climbed to the summit of the Kuenlun mountains. On his return to the southward he lost his magic pearl. He besought his wits to find it, but in vain. He besought his sight to find it, but in vain. He besought his eloquence to find it, but that was also in vain. At last he besought Nothing, and Nothing recovered it. 'How extraordinary!' exclaimed the Yellow Emperor, 'that Nothing should be able to recover it!' Do you understand me, young man?"

"I think this pearl was his soul," I answered, "and that knowledge, sight and speech do but cloud the soul rather than enlighten it; and that it was only in the peace of perfect quietude that his soul's consciousness was restored to the Yellow Emperor. Is it so, Master?"

"Quite right; you have felt it as it is. And do you know, too, by whom this beautiful legend is told?"

"I am young and ignorant; I do not know."

"It is by Chuang-Tse, the disciple of Laotzu, China's greatest philosopher. It was neither Confucius nor Mencius who spoke the purest wisdom in this country, but Laotzu. He was the greatest, and Chuang-Tse was his apostle. You foreigners cherish, I know, a certain well-meaning admiration for Laotzu also, but I think but few of you know that he was the purest human being who ever breathed.—Have you read the 'Tao-Teh-King'? and have you ever considered, I wonder, what he meant by 'Tao'?"

"I should be grateful if you would tell me Master."

"I think I may well instruct you, young man. It is many years since I have had a pupil, and I see in your eyes no curiosity, but rather a pure desire of wisdom, for the freeing of your soul. Listen then. 4

"Tao is really nothing but that which you Westerns call 'God.' Tao is the One; the beginning and the end. It embraces all things, and to it all things return.

"Laotzu wrote at the commencement of his book the sign: Tao. But what he actually meant—the Highest, the One—can have no name, can never be expressed in any sound, just because it is The One. Equally inadequate is your term 'God.'—Wu—Nothing—that is Tao. You do not understand me?—Listen further! There exists, then, an absolute Reality—without beginning, without end—which we cannot comprehend, and which therefore must be to us as Nothing. That which we *are* able to comprehend, which has for us a relative reality, is in truth only appearance. It is an outgrowth, a result of absolute reality, seeing that everything emanates from, and returns to, that reality. But things which are real to us are not real in themselves. What we call Being is in fact Not-Being, and just what we call Not-Being is Being in its true sense. So that we are living in a great obscurity. What we imagine to be real is not real, and yet emanates from the real, for the Real is the Whole. Both Being and Not-Being are accordingly Tao. But above all never forget that 'Tao' is merely a sound uttered by a human being, and that *the idea is essentially inexpressible.*

70

All things appreciable to the senses and all cravings of the heart are unreal. Tao is the source of Heaven and Earth. One begat Two, Two begat Three, Three begat Millions. And Millions return again into One.

"If you remember this well, young man, you have passed the first gateway on the path of Wisdom.

"You know, then, that Tao is the source of everything; of the trees, the flowers, the birds; of the sea, the desert, and the rocks; of light and darkness; of heat and cold; of day and night; of summer and winter, and of your own life. Worlds and oceans evaporate in Eternity. Man rises out of the darkness, laughs in the glimmering light, and disappears. But in all these changes the One is manifested. Tao is in everything. Your soul in her innermost is Tao.—

"You see the world outspread before you, young man? . . ."

With a stately gesture he pointed seawards.

The hills on either side stood fast, uncompromising, clear-set in the atmosphere—like strong thoughts, petrified, hewn out by conscious energy—yielding only in the distance to the tender influence of light and air. On a very high point stood a lonely little tree, of delicate leafage, in a high light. The evening began to fall, with tender serenity; and a rosy glow, dreamy yet brilliant, lent to the mountains, standing ever more sharply defined against it, an air of peaceful joyousness. In it all was to be felt a gentle upward striving, a still poising, as in the rarefied atmosphere of conscious piety. And the sea crept up softly, with a still-swaying slide— with the quiet, irresistible approach of a type of infinity. The sail of a little vessel, gleaming softly golden, glided nearer. So tiny it looked on that immense ocean—so fearless and lovely! All was pure—no trace of foulness anywhere.

And I spoke with the rare impulse of a mighty joy.

"I feel it now, O Master! That which I seek is everywhere. I had no need to seek it in the distance; for it is quite close to me. It is everywhere— what I seek, what I myself am, what my soul is. It is familiar to me as my own self. It is all revelation! God is everywhere! Tao is in everything!"

"That is so, boy, but confuse it not! In that which you see is Tao, but Tao is not what you see. You must not think that Tao is visible to your eyes. Tao will neither waken joy in your heart nor draw your tears. For all your experiences and emotions are relative and not real.

"However, I will speak no more of that at present. You stand as yet but at the first gate, and see but the first glint of dawn. It is already much that you should realize Tao as present in everything. It will render your life more natural and confident—for, believe me, you lie as safe in the arms of Tao as a child in the arms of its mother. And it will make you serious and thoughtful too, for you will feel yourself to be in all places as holy a thing as is a good priest in his temple. No longer will you be frightened by the changes in things, by life and death; for you know that death, as well as life, emanates from Tao. And it is so natural that Tao, which pervaded your life, should also after death continually surround you.

"Look at the landscape before you! The trees, the mountains, the sea, they are your brothers, like the air and the light. Observe how the sea is approaching us! So spontaneously, so naturally, so purely 'because so it must be.'—Do you see your dear sister the little tree on yonder point, bending towards you? and the simple movement of her little leaves?— Then I will speak to you of Wu-Wei, [5] of 'non-resistance,' of 'self-movement' on the breath of your impulse as it was born out of Tao. Men would be true men if they would but let their lives flow of themselves, as the sea heaves, as a flower blooms, in the simple beauty of Tao. In every man there is an impulse towards that movement which, proceeding from Tao, would urge him back to Tao again. But men grow blind through their own senses and lusts. They strive for pleasure, desire, hate, fame and riches. Their movements are fierce and stormy, their progress a series of wild uprisings and violent falls. They hold fast to all that is unreal. They desire too many things to allow of their desiring the One. They desire, too, to be wise and good, and what is worst of all, They desire to know too much.

72

"The one remedy is: the return to the source whence they came. In us is Tao. Tao is rest. Only by renunciation of desire—even the desire for goodness or wisdom—can we attain rest. Oh! all this craving to know what Tao is! And this painful struggle for words in which to express it and to inquire after it!—The truly wise follow the Teaching which is wordless which remains unexpressed. [6] And who shall ever express it? Those who know it (what Tao is) tell it not; those who tell it know it not. [7] Even I shall not tell you what Tao is. Yourself must discover it in that you free yourself from all your passions and cravings, and live in utter spontaneity, void of unnatural striving. Gently must Tao be approached, with a motion reposeful as the movement of that broad ocean. That moves, not because it chooses to move, nor because it knows that it is wise or good to move; it moves involuntarily, unconscious of movement. Thus will you also return to Tao, and when you are returned you will know it not, for you yourself will be Tao."

He ceased speaking, and looked at me gently. His eyes shone with a quiet light, still and even as the tint of the heavens.

"Father," I said, "what you say is beautiful as the sea, and it seems simple as nature; but surely it is not so easy—this strifeless, inactive absorption of man into Tao?"

"Do not confuse words one with another," he replied. "By strifelessness—Wu-Wei—Laotzu did not mean common inaction,—not mere idling, with closed eyes. He meant: relaxation from earthly activity, from desire—from the craving for unreal things. But he *did* exact activity in *real* things. He implied a powerful movement of the soul, which must be freed from its gloomy body like a bird from its cage. He meant a yielding to the inner motive-force which we derive from Tao and which leads us to Tao again. And, believe me: this movement is as natural as that of the cloud above us . . ."

High in the blue ether over our heads were golden clouds, sailing slowly towards the sea. They gleamed with a wonderful purity, as of a high and holy love. Softly, softly they were floating away.

"In a little while they will be gone, vanished in the infinity of the heavens," said the hermit, "and you will see nothing but the eternal blue. Thus will your soul be absorbed into Tao."

"My life is full of sins," I answered; "I am heavily burdened with darkening desires. And so are my benighted fellow-men. How can *our* life ever—thus ethereally, in its purest essence—float towards Tao? It is so heavy with evil, it must surely sink back into the mire."

"Do not believe it, do not believe it!" he exclaimed, smiling in gracious kindliness. "No man can annihilate Tao, and there shines in each one of us the inextinguishable light of the soul. Do not believe that the evilness of humanity is so great and so mighty. The eternal Tao dwells in all; in murderers and harlots as well as in philosophers and poets. All bear within them an indestructible treasure, and not one is better than another. You cannot love the one in preference to the other; you cannot bless the one and damn the other. They are as alike in essence as two grains of sand on this rock. And not one will be banished out of Tao eternally, for all bear Tao within them. Their sins are illusive, having the vagueness of vapours. Their deeds are a false seeming; and their words pass away like ephemeral dreams. They cannot be 'bad,' they cannot be 'good' either. Irresistibly they are drawn to Tao, as yonder waterdrop to the great sea. It may last longer with some than with others, that is all. And a few centuries—what matter they in the face of Eternity?—Poor friend! Has your sin made you so fearful? Have you held your sin to be mightier than Tao? Have you held the sin of men to be mightier than Tao?—You have striven to be good overmuch, and so have seen your own misdoing in a falsely clear light. You have desired overmuch goodness in your fellow-men also, and therefore has their sin unduly troubled you. But all this is a seeming. Tao is neither good nor bad. For Tao is real. Tao alone *is*; and the life of all unreal things is a life of false contrasts and relations, which have no independent existence, and do greatly mislead. So, above all, do not desire to be good, neither call yourself bad. Wu-Wei—unstriving, self-impelled—that must you be. Not bad—not good; not little—and not great; not low—and not high. And only then will you in reality *be*, even whilst, in the ordinary sense you are not. When once you are free from all seeming, from all craving and lusting, then will you move of your own impulse, without so much as knowing that you move; and this, the only true life-principle—this free, untrammelled motion towards Tao—will be light and unconscious as the dissolution of the little cloud above you."

I experienced a sudden sense of freedom. The feeling was not joy—not happiness. It was rather a gentle sense of expansion—a widening of my mental horizon.

"Father," I said, "I thank you! This revelation of Tao lends me already an impulse which, though I cannot explain it, yet seems to bear me gently forward.

"How wonderful is Tao! With all my wisdom—with all my knowledge, I have never felt this before!"

"Crave not thus for wisdom!" said the philosopher. "Do not desire to know too much—so only shall you grow to know intuitively; for the knowledge acquired by unnatural striving only leads away from Tao. Strive not to know all there is to know concerning the men and things around you, nor—and this more especially—concerning their relations and antagonisms. Above all, seek not happiness too greedily, and be not fearful of unhappiness. For neither of these is real. Joy is not real, nor pain either. Tao would not be Tao, were you able to picture it to yourself as pain, as joy, as happiness or unhappiness; for Tao is One Whole, and in it no discords may exist. Hear how simply it is expressed by Chuang-Tse: 'The greatest joy is no joy.' And pain too will have vanished for you! You must never believe pain to be a real thing, an essential element of existence. Your pain will one day vanish as the mists vanish from the mountains. For one day you will realize how natural, how spontaneous are all facts of existence; and all the great problems which have held for you mystery and darkness will become Wu-Wei, quite simple, non-resistant, no longer a source of marvel to you. For everything grows out of Tao, everything is a natural part of the great system developed from a single principle.—Then nothing will have power to trouble you nor to rejoice you more. You will laugh no more, neither will you weep.—I see you look up doubtfully, as though you found me too hard, too cold. Nevertheless, when you are somewhat further advanced you will realize that *this* it means, to be in perfect sympathy with Tao. Then, looking upon 'pain,' you will know that one day it must disappear, because it is unreal; and looking upon 'joy,' you will understand that it is but a primitive and shadowy joy, dependent upon time and circumstance, and deriving its apparent existence from contrast with pain. Looking upon a goodly man, you will find it wholly natural that he should be as he is, and will experience a foreshadowing of how much goodlier he will be in that day when he shall no longer represent the 'kind' and 'good.' And upon a murderer you will look with all calmness, with neither special love nor special hate; for he is your fellow in Tao, and all his sin is powerless to annihilate Tao within him. Then, for the first time, when you are Wu-Wei at last—not, in the common human sense, existing—then all will be well with you, and you will glide through your life as quietly and naturally as the great sea before us. Naught will ruffle your peace. Your sleep will be dreamless, and consciousness of self will bring no care. [8] You will see Tao in all things, be one with all existence, and look round on the whole of nature as on something with which you are intimate as with yourself. And passing with calm acceptance through the changes of day and night, summer and winter, life and death, you will one day enter into Tao, where there is no more change, and whence you issued once as pure as you now return."

"Father, what you say is clear—and compels belief. But life is still so dear to me, and I am afraid of death; I am afraid too lest my friends should die, or my wife, or my child! Death seems to me so black and gloomy—and life is bright—bright—with the sun, and the green and flowery earth!"

"That is because you fail as yet to feel the perfect naturalness of death, which is equal in reality to that of life. You think too much of the insignificant body, and the deep grave in which it must lie; but that is the feeling of a prisoner about to be freed, who is troubled at the thought of leaving the dark cell where he has lived so long. You see death in contrast to life; and both are unreal—both are a changing and a seeming. Your soul does not glide out of a familiar sea into an unfamiliar ocean. That which is real in you, your soul, can never pass away, and this fear is no part of her. You must conquer this fear for ever; or, better still, it will happen when you are older, and have lived spontaneously, naturally, following the motions of Tao, that you will of your own accord cease to feel it . . . Neither will you then mourn for those who have gone home before you; with whom you will one day be reunited—not knowing, yourself, that you are reunited to them, because these contrasts will no longer be apparent to you . . .

". . . It came to pass once upon a time that Chuang-Tse's wife died, and the widower was found by Hui-Tse sitting calmly upon the ground, passing the time, as was his wont, in beating upon a gong. When Hui-Tse rallied him upon the seeming indifference of his conduct, Chuang-Tse replied:

"Thy way of regarding things is unnatural. At first, it is true, I was troubled—I could not be otherwise. But after some pondering I reflected that originally she was not of this life, being not only not born, but without form altogether; and that into this formlessness no life-germ had as yet penetrated. That nevertheless, as in a sun-warmed furrow, life-energy then began to stir; out of life-energy grew form, and form became birth. Today another change has completed itself, and she has died. This resembles the rise and fall of the four seasons: spring, autumn, winter, summer. She sleeps calmly in the Great House. Were I now to weep and wail, it were to act as though the soul of all this had not entered into me,—therefore I do it no more.'" [9]

This he told in a simple, unaffected manner that showed how natural it appeared to him. But it was not yet clear to me, and I said:

"I find this wisdom terrible; it almost makes me afraid. Life would seem to me so cold and empty, were I as wise as this."

"Life *is* cold and empty," he answered, quietly, but with no trace of contempt in his tone;—"and men are as deceptive as life itself. There is not one who knows himself, not one who knows his fellows; and yet they are all alike. There is, in fact, no such thing as life; it is unreal."

I could say no more, and stared before me into the twilight. The mountains were sleeping peacefully in the tender, bloom-like shimmer of vague night-mists—lying lowly, like children, beneath the broad heavens. Below us was an indistinct twinkling of little red lights. From the distance rose a sad monotonous song, the wail of a flute accompanying it. In the depths of the darkness lay the sea in its majesty and the sound of infinitude swelled far and wide.

Then there arose in me a great sadness, and my eyes filled, as with passionate insistence I asked him: "And what of friendship, then?—and what of love?"

He looked at me. I could not see him plainly in the darkness, but there shone from his eyes a curious soft light, and he answered gently:

"These are the best things in life, by very far. They are one with the first stirring of Tao within you. But one day you will know of them as little as the stream knows of its banks when it is lost in the endless ocean. Think not that I would teach you to banish love from your heart; for that would be to go against Tao. Love what you love, and be not misled by the thought that love is a hindrance which holds you in bondage. To banish love from your heart would be a mad and earthly action, and would put you further away from Tao than you have ever been. I say only, that love will one day vanish of itself without your knowing, and that Tao is not Love. But forget not, that—so far as I desire it, and so far as it is good for you—I am speaking to you of the very highest things. Were I only speaking of this life and of men, I should say: Love is the highest of all. But for him who is absorbed again into Tao, love is a thing past and forgotten.

78

"Now, it has grown late, and I would not impart too much to you at first. You will surely desire to sleep within the Temple, and I will prepare your couch. Come with me—and descend the mountain with all caution!"

He lit a little light, and held out his hand to lead me. Slowly we proceeded, step by step. He was as careful of me as though I had been his child; he lighted my path at every steep descent, and led me gently forward, taking heed of all my movements.

When we arrived at the foot, he showed me the little guest-chamber set apart for mandarins, [10] and fetched pillow and covering for me.

"I thank you, Father, from my heart!" I said. "When shall I ever be able to show my gratitude?"

He looked at me quietly, and the glance was great, like the sea. Calm he was, and gentle as night. He smiled at me, and it was like the light laughing upon the earth. And silently he left me.

CHAPTER II

ART

"WHAT is art?" I asked the hermit. We were sitting upon the mountainside, in the shadow of an overhanging rock. Before us stretched the sea—one endless gleam of light in the sunshine. Golden sails were driving quietly over it, and white seagulls sweeping in noble curvings lightly hither and thither, while great, snow-pure clouds came up and sailed by in the blue, majestic in progress, steady and slow.

"It is as natural as the sea—the birds—the clouds," he answered. "I do not think you will find this so hard to grasp and feel as Tao. You have only to look around you—earth, clouds, atmosphere, everything will teach it you. Poetry has existed as long as heaven and earth. [11]

"Beauty was born with the heavens and the earth. The sun, the moon, and the red mists of morning and evening illumine each other, and yet—inexhaustible and wonderful as are the changes presented by them—Nature's great phenomena—there exist no pigments, as for garments, to dye them withal. All phenomena of the world bring forth sound when set in motion, and every sound implies some motion which has caused it. The greatest of all sounds are wind and thunder.

"Listen to the mountain stream racing over the rocks! As soon as it is set in motion the sound of it—high or low, short or long—makes itself heard, not actually according to the laws of music, it is true, yet having a certain rhythm and system.

"This is the spontaneous voice of heaven and earth; the voice that is caused by movement.

"Well! In the purest state of the human heart—when the fire of the spirit is at its brightest—then, if it be moved, that too will give forth sound. Is it not a wondrous metamorphosis that out of this a literature should be created?"

"So Poetry is the sound of the heart?"

"You will feel how natural this is. Poetry is to be heard and seen everywhere, for the whole of Nature is one great poet. But just because of its simplicity, therefore is it so strict and unalterable. Where the spring of movement is, there flows the sound of the poem. Any other sound is no poetry. The sound must come quite of itself—Wu-Wei—it cannot be generated by any artifices. There are many—how many!—who by unnatural movement force forth sound; but these are no poets—rather do they resemble apes and parrots. Few indeed are the true poets. From these the verse flows of itself, full of music,—powerful as the roaring of the torrent amongst the rocks, as the rolling of thunder in the clouds,—soft as the swishing of an evening shower, or the gentle breath of a summer night-breeze.—Hark! hark to the sea at our feet! Is it not singing a wondrous song? Is it not a very poem?—is it not pure music? See how the waves sway, in ceaseless mobility—one after the other— one over the other—swinging onward and onward—ever further and further—returning to vanish in music once more! Dost thou hear their rhythmic rushing? Oh! great and simple must a poet be—like the sea! His movement, like that of the sea, is an impulse out of Tao, and in that—tranquil, strifeless, obedient as a child—must he let himself go. Great, great is the sea! Great, great is the poet. But greater—greater—is Tao, that which is not great!"

He was silent, listening to the sea, and I saw how the music of it entered into him.

I had reflected much since hearing his first words concerning Tao. I was fearful lest his great and lofty philosophy should mean death to the artist, and that I also, in giving myself over to this wisdom of his, should become incapable of feeling the inspiration of the poet, and of being any more childishly enraptured at the sight of beauty.

But he himself was standing there in the purest ecstasy, as though he were now looking upon the sea for the first time; and reverently, with shining eyes, he listened to the rush of the waves. "Is it not beautiful?" he said again, "is it not beautiful,—this sound, that came out of Tao, the soundless?—this light, that shone out of Tao, the lightless? and the word-music: verse, born of Tao the wordless? Do we not live in an endless mystery?—resolving one day into absolute truth!"

I was a long time silent. But its very simplicity was hard for me to grasp. And I asked him doubtfully: "Can it really be so easy—to make and sing poems? It is surely not so easy for us to bring forth verse as for the stream to rush over the rocks? Must we not first practise and train ourselves, and learn to know the verse-forms thoroughly? And is not that voluntary action, rather than involuntary motion?"

My question did not embarrass him, and he answered at once:—

"Do not let that perplex you. All depends on whether a man has in him the true spring from which the verse should flow, or not. Has he the pure impulse from Tao within him? or is his life-motive something less simply beautiful? If he *has* that source in him he is a poet, if he has it not he is none. By this time you surely realize that, considered from a high standpoint, all men are really poets; for, as I have told you, there exists in all men the essential, original impulse emanating from and returning to Tao. But rarely do we find this impulse alert and strongly developed—rarely are men endowed with perception of the higher revelations of beauty, through which their bank-bound life-stream flows till lost in boundless eternity. One might express it thus: that ordinary men are like still water in swampy ground, in the midst of poor vegetation; while poets are clear streams, flowing amidst the splendour of luxuriant banks to the endless ocean. But I would rather not speak so much in symbols, for that is not plain enough.

82

"You would fain know whether a man who *has* the true inspiration of the poet must not nevertheless train himself somewhat in his art, or whether he moves in it entirely of himself, like nature?—The latter is without doubt the case! For a young poet, having studied verse-form in all its variety for but a short time, suddenly comes to find these forms so natural as to preclude his inclination for any other. His verse assumes beautiful form involuntarily, simply because other movement would be alien. That is just the difference between the poet and the dilettante: that the poet sings his verse spontaneously, from his own impulse, and afterwards, proving it, finds it to be right in sound—in rhythm—in all its movement; whereas the dilettante, after first marking out for himself a certain verse-form, according to the approved pattern of the art-learned, proceeds to project by main force a series of wholly soulless words upon it. The soulful words of the poet flowed of themselves just because they were soulful. And, if we view things in their true light, there do actually exist *no* hard and fast forms for poetry, and absolutely no laws; for a verse which flows spontaneously from its source moves of itself, and is independent of all preconceived human standards! The one law is that there shall be no law. Mayhap you will find this over-daring, young man! But remember that my demonstrations are taken not from men, but out of Tao, and that I know, moreover, but very few true poets. The man who is simple and pure as Nature is rare indeed. Think you that there are many such in your own land?"

This unexpected question embarrassed me, and I wondered what could be his drift. It was hard to answer, too, so I asked him first another question:

"Great Master, I cannot answer until I hear more from you. *Why does* a poet make a poem?"

That seemed to astonish him mightily, for he repeated it, as though doubting if he had heard aright:

"Why does a poet make a poem?"

"Yes, Master, why?"

Then he laughed outright, and said:

"Why does the sea roar? Why does the bird sing? Do you know that, my son?"

"Because they cannot help it, Father, because they simply must give their nature vent in that way! It is Wu-Wei!"

"Quite so! Well,—and why should it be different with a poet?"

I considered, and my answer came none too readily.

"Yes, but it *may* be different. A poet may sing for the sake of creating or enriching a literature, where there is none, or it is in danger of dying out. That has a fine sound, but is no pure motive. Or some poets sing in order to cover themselves with glory—to be famous, to be crowned with shining laurels, and to gain smiles from the fair, bright-eyed maidens strewing flowers on the path before them!"

"You must express yourself with greater exactness," said the hermit, "and not desecrate words which thousands hold sacred. For poets who sing for such reasons are no poets at all. A poet sings because he sings. He cannot sing with any given purpose, or he becomes a dilettante."

"Then, Father, supposing a poet to have sung as simply as a bird, may he afterwards take pleasure in the laurels and the roses? May he jealously hate those who wear the laurels of which he deems himself worthy? or can he believe his soul's convictions, and call beauty ugly, despising the beauty which he has created?—Can he call the beautiful hateful, because the laurels come from unwelcome hands?—Can he drape himself in a false garb, and elect to act differently from other men, in order to gain prominence through eccentricity?—Can he deem himself better than the common run of men?—Should he press the common hands which applaud him?—May he hate them who deride instead of honouring him?—How can you interpret to me all these things? They all appear so strange to me, in comparison with the little bird and the great sea!"

"All these questions, young friend, are an answer to *my* question," he replied; "for the fact that you would know all this is a proof that there are not many poets in your country. Remember that I understand and use the word 'poet' in its purest, highest meaning. A poet can only live for his art, which he loves for itself, and not as a means for securing fleeting earthly pleasures. A poet looks upon men and things—in their nature and relationship—so simply, that he himself approaches very nearly to the nature of Tao. Other men see men and things hazily, as through a fog. The poet realizes this to be an incontestable fact. How then can he expect his simplicity to be understood—by this hazy mind of the public? How can he cherish feelings of hate and grief when it ridicules him? How feel pleasure when it should do him honour? It is the same in this case as with the four 'seasons' of Chuang-Tse. There is nothing specially agitating in it all, because it is the natural course of things. Consequently the poet is neither in despair when he is not heard, nor happy when he is fêted. He looks upon the state of things with regard to the multitude and the way it comports itself towards him as a natural consequence, of which he knows the cause. The judgment of the common people is not even so much as indifferent to him—it simply does not exist for him. He does not sing his verses for the sake of the people, but because he cannot help himself. The sound of human comment on his work escapes him entirely, and he knows not whether he be famous or forgotten. 'The highest fame is no fame.' * You look at me, young man, as though I were telling stranger things than you have ever dared to dream. But I am telling nothing but the plainest truth, simple and natural as the truth in landscape or sea. Having dwelt until so lately mid the strenuous life of your countrymen, you have never yet seen true simplicity. For so long you have heard nothing spoken of but 'fame,' 'earnings,' 'honour,' 'artists' and 'immortality,' that, for all you know, these things may be indispensable as air, and veritable as your soul. But it is all a seeming and deception. Those whom you have seen may indeed have been poets of true fibre, but they had been led astray from the impulse derived from Tao which was their life-principle, and they did not remain what they

---

*   From the "Nan Hwa King," chap. xviii.

were, but sank through their weakness to the nature of commonplace men. So that they have come to do as ordinary men do, only they do it more strongly. So much do I gather from your questioning. But all these are poets no longer, and will sing no more true poetry so long as they remain as they are. For the smallest deviation from the original impulse is sufficient to kill the poetry within them. There is but the one direct way: single and simple as a maiden—uncompromising as a straight line. This straight line is spontaneity; on either side of it lie false activity and the unnatural—also the roads to fame and notoriety, where occur murder, and sudden death, and where one bosom friend will suck the life-blood from another to further the attainment of his own ends. The straight line cuts its own way, without deviation or secret windings, in simple continuance into infinity.

"You understand then, that thus, by the nature of things, all those situations which would convert the poet into the sacrificial victim of the mob become impossible. You have probably read, in the history alike of your country and my own, of poets who have died of grief at want of recognition, or who have taken their own lives on account of undeserved contumely. I have indeed always felt the pathos of this, yet have realized that to such poets as these the tern truly great cannot be applied.

"And I am speaking, of course, not of the artists of speech only, but of all artists. Shall I show you now something by an artist as true and simple-minded as I can conceive a man to be?—Come with me then!"

He led me into a small chamber in his hut—a cell with white walls and no furniture save the bed, a table covered with books, and a few chairs. He opened a door in the wall, and drew out from it a wooden chest. This he carried as carefully as though it had been some sacred object or a little child. He set it gently down upon the floor, opened the lid, and lifted out a closed shrine of red-brown wood, which he placed upon the table. [12]

"See," he remarked, "this is a beautiful shrine, to begin with. A beautiful thing must have a beautiful setting. At present the little doors are shut. Do you not find this a goodly idea: to be able ever thus to hold it hidden from profane eyes?—But before *you* I may well open it."

And the two wings of the shrine flew apart.

Against a background of pale blue silk appeared a large figure, gleaming, and shimmering, and diffusing a wonderful radiance of its own. It was the Buddha Kwan Yin, seated upon a lotus that reared itself, straight, and graceful, and modestly opened, above a tumult of wild waves. [13]

"Do you perceive the utter simplicity and beauty of this?" he asked me; and in his voice there spoke a great and tender love. "Is not this the very embodiment of perfect rest?—How serene is the countenance— how wonderfully tender, and yet how tensely grave, with its closed eyes gazing into infinity!—See—the cheek,—how delicate and tender! See— the mouth—and the lofty curving of the eyebrows—and the pure pearl gleaming above her forehead [14]—symbol of a soul taking its flight from the body! And the body—how few are the lines of it! Yet see: what infinite love and mercifulness in the downward pose of the left arm; and in the uplifted right arm—with two raised fingers, held together as in the act of preaching—what an indescribable holiness! And how beautiful the repose of the crossed legs resting so softly upon the lotus!—And see—how tenderly felt, notwithstanding the immense strength and restraint of the whole—the delicate soles of the feet, curved with such subtle gentleness!—Is it not the quintessence of the whole of Buddhism in a single picture? You need no to have read anything of Buddhism in order to appreciate it now, here, in all its inmost meaning. Rest— is it not absolute rest—this ideally pure countenance gazing thus stilly into eternity? Love—is it not absolute love for the world—this simple drooping of the arm? And is not the essence of the whole doctrine grasped and confined in the pose of the uplifted fingers?

"And then—the material of which such a figure as this is made! Do you realize, I wonder, that an artist such as this must have laboured for years and years before his material became as pure and ethereal as he required it to be? For the nature of stone is so hard—is it not?—and the general idea of it: matter—that would suit but ill for the plastic representation of the ideal conception: Rest.—So the artist wrought upon all kinds of common materials such as clay, sand, and earth, and transformed them, by means of fit and harmonious combination with precious stones, pearls, and jasper, into costly substances. And so the material for this figure became something that was no longer material, but rather the incarnation of a sublime idea. The artist wished to symbolize also in his representation the rosy dawn which broke upon mankind on the appearance of Buddha; and so, shimmering through the snowy white of his porcelain, he introduced just such a vague rosy glow as plays upon the morning clouds before the glory of the sun bursts forth. Is not this half-realized, .growing light more instinct with feeling than light itself? Can you perceive this most indefinite, yet clear and rosy colour shimmering throughout the white? Is it not chaste as the first soft blush of a maiden? Is it not the godly love of the artist which thus glows in the pureness of the white? Such a figure is, in fact, no longer a figure. The idea of material is entirely obliterated; it is an inspiration."

For a long time I was too much moved to speak. More strongly yet than the pure wisdom of the old man, did the beauty of this art take hold upon and purify my soul. At last I asked gently:

"Who has created this marvel? I would fain know, that I may hold his name with yours in veneration."

"That is of little importance, my young friend!" he answered. "The soul that was in this artist is absorbed again into Tao, just as yours will be one day. His body has fallen away, like the leaves from a tree, just as yours in time will fall away. What weight can attach then to his name? Nevertheless, I will tell it you; he was called Tan Wei, [15] and he engraved this name in finely-devised characters upon the back of the figure, such being the custom at that time.—Who was he? A common workman, surely, who did not even know, himself, that he was an artist; who seemed to himself nothing more than a common peasant, and who had not the least suspicion that his work was so beautiful. But he must have gazed much at the heavens and clouds above him, and have loved the wide seas, and the landscapes, and the flowers; otherwise he could not have been so fine in feeling; for such simple lines and pure colours are only to be found in Nature. He was certainly not celebrated; you will not find his name in any history. I could not tell you whence he came, how he lived, or to what age. I know only that it is more than four hundred years since such figures as these were made, and that connoisseurs reckon that this one dates from the first half of the Ming-Dynasty. Most probably the artist lived quite quietly the same sort of life as the other people, worked industriously as a common labourer, and died humbly, unconscious of his own greatness. But his work remained, and this image, which by a fortunate chance has found its way to this district, where the last wars never raged, is still the same as when he made it. And thus it may last on for centuries and centuries, in inextinguishable radiance, in maidenly majesty. O, to create such a thing, in pure, unconscious simplicity—that is to be a poet! That is the art which dates not from time but from eternity!—How beautiful it is! Do you not find it so too? This porcelain, that is almost indestructible; this radiance, which never dies away! Here upon the earth it stands, so strong and yet so tender, and so it will be, long after our successors are dead!—And the soul of the artist is with Tao!"

We continued long to look upon the image. Then he took careful hold of the shrine once more. "It is so delicate," he said, "that I hardly dare to expose it to broad daylight. For this miracle of tenderness—ethereal as a soul—the daylight is too hard. I feel a kind of anxiety lest the light should suddenly break it in pieces; or cause it to dissolve like a little light cloud—so wholly soul-like is its composition!"

And softly, very softly, he replaced the shrine within the chest, which he closed.

He went out now, before me, and we seated our'-selves again beneath the overhanging rock.

"How beautiful it would be," I said, "if every one could make things like that, in all simplicity, and surround themselves with them, everywhere!"

"Every one!" he answered; "well, that is perhaps too much to expect! But there really was once a time when this great kingdom was one great temple of art and beauty. You may still see the traces of it here in China. At that time the greater number of the people were simple-minded artists. All objects surrounding them were beautiful, the smallest thing as well as the greatest—whether it were a temple, a garden, a table, a chair, or a knife. Just examine the little teacups, or the smallest censers of that period! The poorest coolie ate out of vessels as perfect in their way as my Kwan-Yin image. All objects were beautifully made, and involuntarily so. The simple artisans did not consider themselves 'artists,' or in any way different from their fellow-men, and no petty strife can have arisen between them, otherwise there would have been an end of their art. Everything was beautiful because they were all single-minded and worked honestly. It was as natural in those days for things to be beautiful as it is now-a-days for them to be ugly. The art of China has sunk to its lowest ebb; that is a consequence of its miserable social condition. You have surely remarked that the art of the country is deteriorating. And that is a death-sign for this great Empire. For Art is inseparably connected with the full-bloom of a country's life. If the art declines, then the whole country degenerates. I do not mean this in the political, but rather in the moral sense. For a morally-strong and simple-hearted people brings forth involuntarily a strong and healthy art.—Yes, what you said is true; how much better would men's lives be, could they but create for themselves better surroundings! And how extraordinary that this is not done! For Nature remains ever and everywhere accessible to them. See the clouds—the trees—the sea!"

The sea was still, as ever, splashing at our feet—boundless and pure. Clouds sailed majestically landwards, with a slow motion, in the full blaze of the light. Golden gleams, falling upon the mountains, vanished again with the rhythmical sweep of the clouds. Light and motion, sound and play of colour, everywhere!

The hermit gazed calmly and confidingly at this infinite loveliness; as though deeply conscious of the intimate relationship existing between him and all his surroundings. He seemed to guess what was in my mind as I looked at him, for he said:

"We fit as naturally into this beauty around us as a tree or a mountain. If we can but remain so always, we shall retain the feeling of our own well-being amid all the great workings of the world-system. So much has been said about human life; and scholars have created such an endless labyrinth of theories! And yet in its inmost kernel it is as plain as Nature. All things are equal in simplicity, and nothing is really in confusion, however much it may seem as though it were so. Everything moves surely and inevitably as the sea."

There rang in his voice both the great love of the poet and the quiet assurance of the scholar who takes his stand upon incontrovertible truth.

"Are you satisfied for today?" was his friendly question; "and have I helped you forward a little? Do you feel more clearly what poetry is?"

"Father," I answered, "your wisdom is poetry, and your poetry is wisdom! How can that be?"

"That is quite true, from your point of view," he answered. "But you have yet to learn that all these words are but a seeming. I know not what my wisdom is, nor my poetry. It is all one. It is so simple and natural when you understand this! It is all Tao."

CHAPTER III

LOVE

ONCE more it was evening. We sat again upon the soft turf of the mountain-side, the quietness of our mood in sympathy with the solemn stillness of twilight. The distant mountain-ranges reposed in an atmosphere breathing reverence and devotion—they seemed to be kneeling beneath the heavens, beneath the slow-descending blessing of night. The isolated trees dotted here and there about the hills stood motionless, in a pause of silent worshipping. The rush of the sea sounded distant and indistinct, lost in its own greatness. Peace lay over everything, and soft sounds went up, as of prayer.

The hermit stood before me, dignified as a tree in the midst of Nature, and awe-inspiring as the evening itself.

I had returned to question him again. For my soul found no repose apart from him, and a mighty impulse was stirring within me. But now that I found myself near him, I hardly dared to speak; and indeed it seemed as though words were no longer necessary—as though everything lay, of itself, open and clear as daylight. How goodly and simple everything appeared that evening! Was it not my own inmost being that I recognized in all the beauty around me? and was not the whole on the point of being absorbed into the Eternal?

Nevertheless I broke in upon this train of feeling, and cleft the peaceful silence with my voice:

"Father," I said sadly, "all your words have sunk into my mind, and my soul is filled with the balm of them. This soul of mine is no longer my own—no longer what I used to be. It is as though I were dead: and I know not what is taking place within me—by day and by night—causing it to grow so light, and clear, and vacant in my mind. Father, I know it is Tao; it is death, and glorious resurrection; but it is not love; and without love, Tao appears to me but a gloomy lie."

The old man looked round him at the evening scene, and smiled gently.

"What *is* love?" he asked calmly. "Are you sure about that, I wonder?"

"No, I am not sure," I answered. "I do not know anything about it, but that is just the reason of its great blessedness. Yes, do but let me express it! I mean: love of a Maiden, love of a woman.—I remember yet, Father, what it was to me when I saw the maiden, and my soul knew delight for the first time. It was like a sea, like a broad heaven, like death. It was light—and I had been blind! It hurt, Father—my heart beat so violently—and my eyes burned. The world was a fire, and all things were strange, and began to live. It was a great flame flaring from out my soul. It was so fearful, but so lovely, and so infinitely great! Father, I think it was greater than Tao!"

"I know well what it was," said the sage. "It was Beauty, the earthly form of the formless Tao, calling up in you the rhythm of that movement by which you will enter into Tao. You might have experienced the same at sight of a tree, a cloud, a flower. But because you are human, living by desire, therefore to you it could only be revealed through another human being, a woman—because, also, that form is to you more easily understood, and more familiar. And since desire did not allow the full upgrowth of a pure contemplation, therefore was the rhythm within you wrought up to be wild tempest, like a storm-thrashed sea that knows not whither it is tending. The inmost essence of the whole emotion was not 'love,' but Tao."

But the calmness of the old sage made me impatient, and excited me to answer roughly:

"It is easy to talk thus theoretically, but seeing that you have never experienced it yourself, you can understand nothing of that of which you speak!"

He looked at me steadily, and laid his hand sympathetically on my shoulder.

"It would be cruel of you to speak thus to any one but me, young man!—I loved, before you drew breath in this world! At that time there lived a maiden, so wondrous to see, it was as if she were the direct-born expression of Tao. For me she was the world, and the world lay dead around her. I saw nothing but her, and for me there existed no such things as trees, men, or clouds. She was more beautiful than this evening, gentler than the lines of those distant mountains, more tender than those hushed tree-tops; and the light of her presence was more blessed to see than the still shining of yonder star. I will not tell you her story. It was more scorching than a very hell-fire—but it was not real, and it is over now, like a storm that has passed. It seemed to me that I must die; I longed to flee from my pain into death.—But there came a dawning in my soul, and all grew light and comprehensible. Nothing was lost. All was yet as it had been. The beauty which I believed to have been taken from me lived on still, spotless, in myself. For not from this woman,—out of my soul had this beauty sprung; and this I saw shining yet, all over the world, with an everlasting radiance, Nature was no other than what I had fashioned to myself out of that shadowy form of a woman. And my soul was one with Nature, and floated with a like rhythm towards the eternal Tao."

Calmed by his calmness, I said: "She whom I loved is dead, Father— She who culled my soul as a child culls a flower never became my wife. But I have a wife now, a miracle of strength and goodness, a wife who is essential to me as light and air. I do not love her as I even now love the dead. But I know that she is a purer human being than that other. How is it then that I do *not* love her so much? She has transformed my wild and troubled life into a tranquil march towards death. She is simple and true as Nature itself, and her face is dear to me as the sunlight."

"You love her, indeed!" said the sage, "but you know not what love means, nor loving. I will tell it you. Love is no other than the rhythm of Tao. I have told you: you are come out of Tao, and to Tao you will return. Whilst you are young—with your soul still enveloped in darkness—in the shock of the first impulse within you, you know not yet whither you are trending. You see the woman before you. You believe her to be that towards which the rhythm is driving you. But even when the woman is yours, and you have thrilled at the touch of her, you feel the rhythm yet within you, unappeased, and know that you must forward, ever further, if you would bring it to a standstill. Then it is that in the soul of the man and of the woman there arises a great sadness, and they look at one another, questioning whither they are now bound. Gently they clasp one another by the hand, and move on through life, swayed by the same impulse, towards the same goal. Call this love if you will. What is a name? I call it Tao. And the souls of those who love are like two white clouds floating softly side by side, that vanish, wafted by the same wind, into the infinite blue of the heavens."

"But that is not the love that I mean!" I cried. "Love is not the desire to see the loved one absorbed into Tao; love is the longing to be always with her; the deep yearning for the blending of the two souls in one; the hot desire to soar, in one breath with her, into felicity! And this always with the loved one alone—not with others, not with Nature. And, were I absorbed into Tao, all this happiness would be for ever lost! Oh let me stay here, in this goodly world, with my faithful companion! Here it is so bright and homely, and Tao is still so gloomy and inscrutable for me."

"The hot desire dies out," he answered calmly. "The body of your loved one will wither and pass away within the cold earth. The leaves of the trees fade in autumn, and the withered flowers droop sadly to the ground. How can you love that so much which does not last? However, you know, in truth, as yet, neither how you love nor what it is that you love. The beauty of woman is but a vague reflection of the formless beauty of Tao. The emotion it awakens, the longing to lose yourself in her beauty, that ecstasy of feeling which would lend wings for the flight of your soul with the beloved—beyond horizon-bounds, into regions of bliss—believe me, it is no other than the rhythm of Tao; only you know it not. You resemble still the river which knows as yet only its shimmering banks; which has no knowledge of the power that draws it forward; but which will one day inevitably flow out into the great ocean. Why this striving after happiness, after human happiness, that lasts but a moment and then vanishes again? Chuang-Tse said truly: 'The highest happiness is no happiness.' Is it not small and pitiable, this momentary uprising, and downfalling, and uprising again? This wavering, weakly intention and progress of men? Do not seek happiness in a woman. She is the joyful revelation of Tao directed towards you. She is the purest form in the whole of nature by which Tao is manifested. She is the gentle force that awakens the rhythm of Tao within you. But she is only a poor creature like yourself. And you are for her the same joyful revelation that she is to you. Fancy not that that which you perceive in her is that Tao, that very holiest, into which you would one day ascend! For then you would surely reject her when you realized what she was. If you will truly love a woman, then love her as being of the same poor nature as yourself, and do not seek happiness with her. Whether in your love you see this or not—her inmost being is Tao. A poet looks upon a woman, and, swayed by the 'rhythm,' he perceives the beauty of the beloved in all things—in the trees, the mountains, the horizon; for the beauty of a woman is the same as that of Nature. It is the form of Tao, the great and formless, and what your soul desires in the excitement of beholding—this strange, unspeakable feeling—is nothing but your oneness with this beauty, and with the source of this beauty—Tao. And the like is experienced by your wife. Ye are for each other angels, who lead one another to Tao unconsciously."

I was silent for a while, reflecting. In the soft colouring and stillness of the evening lay a great sadness. About the horizon, where the sun had set, there glimmered a streak of faint red light, like dying pain.

"What is this sadness, then, in the Nature around us?" I asked. "Is there not that in the twilight as though the whole earth were weeping with a grievous longing? See how she mourns, with these fading hues, these drooping tree-tops, and solemn mountains. Human eyes must fill with tears, when this great grief of Nature looms within their sight. It is as though she were longing for her beloved—as though everything—seas, mountains and heavens—were full of mourning.

And the Sage replied: "It is the same pain which cries in the hearts of men. Your own longing quivers in Nature too. The 'Heimweh' of the evening is also the 'Heimweh' of your soul. Your soul has lost her love: Tao, with whom she once was one; and your soul desires re-union with her love. Absolute re-union with Tao—is not that an immense love?—to be so absolutely one with the beloved that you are wholly hers, she wholly yours;—a union so full and eternal that neither death nor life can ever cleave your oneness again? So tranquil and pure that desire can no more awaken in you—perfect blessedness being attained, and a holy and permanent peace? . . . For Tao is one single, eternal, pure infinitude of soul.

"Is that not more perfect than the love of a woman?—this poor, sad love, each day of which reveals to you some sullying of the clear life of the soul by dark and sanguine passion? When you are absorbed into Tao, then only will you be completely, eternally united with the soul of your beloved, with the souls of all men, your brothers, and with the soul of Nature. And the few moments of blessedness fleetingly enjoyed by all lovers upon earth are as nothing in comparison with that endless bliss: the blending of the souls of all who love in an eternity of perfect purity."

A horizon of blessedness opened out before my soul, wider than the vague horizon of the sea, wider than the heavens.

"Father!" I cried in ecstasy, "can it be that everything is so holy, and I have never known it?—I have been so filled with longing, and so wornout with weeping; and my breast has been heavy with sobs and dread. I have been so consumed with fear! I have trembled at the thought of death! I have despaired of all things being good, when I saw so much suffering around me. I have believed myself damned, by reason of the wild passions, the bodily desires, burning within and flaming without me—passions which, though hating them, I still was, coward-like, condemned to serve. With what breathless horror I have realized how the tender, flower-like body of my love must one day moulder and crumble away in the cold, dark earth! I have believed that I should never feel again that blessed peace at the look in her eyes, through which her soul was shining. And was it Tao!—was Tao really even then always within me, like a faithful guardian? and was it Tao that shone from her eyes? Was Tao in everything that surrounded me? in the clouds, the trees and the sea? Is the inmost being of earth and heaven, then, also the inmost being of my beloved and my own soul? Is it *that* for which there burns within me that mysterious longing which I did not understand, and which drove me so restlessly onward? I thought it was leading me away from the beloved and that I was ceasing to love her!—Was it really the rhythm of Tao, then, that moved my beloved too?—the same as that in which all nature breathes, and all suns and planets pursue their shining course throughout eternity?—Then all is indeed made holy!—then Tao is indeed in everything, as my soul is in Tao! Oh, Father, Father! it is growing so light in my heart! My soul seems to foresee that which will come one day; and the heavens above us, and the great sea, they foretell it too! See, how reverent is the pose of these trees around us—and see the lines of the mountains, how soft in their holy repose! All Nature is filled with sacred awe, and my soul too thrills with ecstasy, for she has looked upon her beloved!"

I sat there long, in silent, still forgetfulness. It was to me as though I were one with the soul of my master and with Nature. I saw nothing and heard nothing;—void of all desire, bereft of all will, I lay sunk in the deepest peace. I was awakened by a soft sound close by me. A fruit had fallen from the tree to the ground behind us. When I looked up, it was into shimmering moonlight. The recluse was standing by me, and bent over me kindly.

"You have strained your spirit overmuch, my young friend!" he said concernedly. "It is too much for you in so short a time. You have fallen asleep from exhaustion. The sea sleeps too. See, not a furrow breaks its even surface; motionless, dreaming, it receives the benediction of the light. But you must awaken! It is late, your boat is ready, and your wife awaits you at home in the town."

I answered, still half dreaming: "I would so gladly stay here. Let me return, with my wife, and stay here for ever! I cannot go back to the people again! Ah, Father, I shudder—I can see their scoffing faces, their insulting glances, their disbelief, and their irreverence! How can I retain the wondrous light and tender feeling of my soul in the midst of that ungracious people? How can I ever so hide it under smile or speech that they shall never detect it, nor desecrate it with their insolent ridicule?"

Then, laying his hand earnestly upon my shoulder, he said:

"Listen carefully to what I now say to you, my friend, and above all, *believe* me. I shall give you pain, but I cannot help it. You *must* return to the world and your fellow-men; it cannot be otherwise. You have spoken too much with me already; perhaps I have said somewhat too much to you. Your further growth must be your own doing, and you must find out everything for yourself. Be only simple of heart, and you will discover everything without effort, like a child finding flowers. At this moment you feel deeply and purely what I have said to you. This present mood is one of the highest moments of your life. But you cannot yet be strong enough to maintain it. You will relapse, and spiritual feeling will turn again to words and theories. Only by slow degrees will you grow once more to feel it purely and keep it permanently. When that is so, then you may return hither in peace and then you will do well to remain here;—but by that time I shall be long dead.

"You must complete your growth in the midst of life, not outside it; for you are not yet pure enough to rise above it. A moment ago, it is true, you were equal even to that, but the reaction will soon set in. You may not shun the rest of mankind; they are your equals, even though they may not feel. so purely as you do. You can go amongst them as their comrade, and take them by the hand; only do not let them look upon your soul, so long as they are still so far behind you. They would not mock you from evilmindedness, but rather out of religious persuasion, being unaware how utterly miserable, how godless, how forsaken they are, and how far from all those holy things by which you actually live. You must be so strong in your conviction that nothing can hinder you. And that you will only become after a long and bitter struggle. But out of your tears will grow your strength, and through pain you will attain peace. Above all remember that Tao, Poetry and Love are one and the same, although you may seek to define it by these several vague terms;—that it is always within you and around you;—that it never forsakes you; and that you are safe and well cared for in this holy environment. You are surrounded with benefits, and sheltered by a love which is eternal. Everything is rendered holy through the primal force of Tao dwelling within it." He spoke so gently and convincingly that I had no answer to give. Willingly I allowed myself to be guided by him to the shore. My boat lay motionless upon the smooth water, awaiting me.—

"Farewell, my young friend! Farewell!" he said, calmly and tenderly. "Remember all that I have told you!"

But I could not leave him in such a manner. Suddenly I thought of the loneliness of his life in this place, and tears of sympathy rose to my eyes. I grasped his hand.

"Father, come with me!" I besought him. "My wife and I will care for you; we will do everything for you; and when you are sick we will tend you. Do not stay here in this loneliness, so void of all the love that might make life sweet to you!"

100

He smiled gently, and shook his head as a father might at some fancy of his child's, answering with tranquil kindness:

"You have lapsed already! Do you realize now how necessary it is for you to remain in the midst of the every-day life? I have but this moment told you how great is the love which surrounds me—and still you deem me lonely here and forsaken?—Here, in Tao, I am as safe at home as a child is with its mother. You mean it well, my friend, but you must grow wiser, much wiser! Be not concerned for me; that is unnecessary, grateful though I am to you for this feeling. Think of yourself just now. And do what I say. Believe that I tell you that which is best for you. In the boat lies something which should remind you of the days you have spent here. Farewell!"

I bent silently over his hand and kissed it. I thought I felt that it trembled with emotion; but when I looked at him again his face was calm and cheerful as the moon in the sky.

I stepped into the boat, and the boatman took up the oars. With dextrous strokes he drove it over the even surface of the water. I was already some way from the land when my foot struck against some object in the boat and I remembered that something for me was lying there. I took it up. It was a small chest. Hastily I lifted the lid. And in the soft, calm moonlight there gleamed with mystical radiance the wonderful porcelain of the Kwan-Yin image, the same which the old man had cherished so carefully, and loved so well.

There, in the lofty tranquillity of severe yet gentle lines, in all the ethereal delicacy of the transparent porcelain, reposed the pure figure of Kwan-Yin, shining as with spiritual radiance amidst the shimmering petals of the lotus.

I scarcely dared believe that this holy thing had been given to me. I seized my handkerchief, and waved with it towards the shore, to convey to the recluse my thanks. He stood there motionless, gazing straight before him. I waited longingly for him to wave—for one more greeting from him—one more sign of love—but he remained immovable.

101

Was it I after whom he was gazing? Was he gazing at the sea? . . .

I closed the lid of the chest, and kept it near me, as though it had been a love of his which I was bearing away. I knew now that he cared for me; but his imperturbable serenity was too great for me—it saddened my mood that he had never signed to me again.

We drew further and further away; the outlines of his figure grew fainter and fainter; at last I could see it no more.

He remained; with the dreams of his soul, in the midst of Nature—alone in infinity—bereft of all human love—but close to the great bosom of Tao.

I took my way back to the life amongst mankind, my brothers and equals—in all the souls of whom dwells Tao, primordial and eternal.

The ornamental lights of the harbour gleamed already in the distance, and the drone of the great town sounded nearer and nearer to us over the sea.

Then I felt a great strength in me, and I ordered the boatman to row still more quickly. I was ready. Was I not as safely and well cared for in the great town as in the still country?—in the street as on the sea?

In everything, everywhere, dwells Poetry—Love—Tao. And the whole world is a great sanctuary, well-devised and surely-maintained as a strong, well-ordered house.

NOTES

1. This is a fact. Chinese priests are in the habit of repeating Sutras which, to judge by the sound, have been translated from the Sanscrit into Chinese phrases of which they do not understand one word.
2. The "Yellow Emperor" is a legendary emperor, who appears to have reigned about the year 2697 B.C.
3. That which follows in inverted commas is an extract translated from the twelfth chapter of the "Nan Hwa King."
4. The following passage, as far as the sentence "and the Millions return again into One" is an adaptation—not a translation—of the first section of "Tao-Teh-King." Laotsu's wonderfully simple writing cannot possibly be translated into equally simple passages in our language. This rendering of mine—arrived at partly by aid of Chinese commentators—is an entirely new reading, and is, to the best of my knowledge, the true one. One of the most celebrated, and in a certain sense, one of the most competent of the sinologues, Herbert Giles, translates of this first section only the first sentence, and finds the rest not worth the trouble of translating! (compare "The Remains of Lao Tzü," by H. A. Giles, Honkong, *China Mail Office*, 1886). This same scholar translates "Tao" as "the Way," not perceiving how impossible it is that that which Laotsu meant—the highest of all, the infinite—should be a "way," seeing that a way (in the figurative sense) always leads to something else, and therefore cannot be the highest. Another still more celebrated sinologue, Dr. Legge, translates "Tao" as "Course," and out of the simple sentence: "If Tao could be expressed in words it would not be the eternal Tao" he makes: "The Course that can be trodden is not the enduring and unchanging course." The whole secret is this: that the sign or word "Tao" has a great number of meanings, and that in Confucius's work "Chung Yung" it does as a matter of fact mean "Way"; but in a hundred other instances it means: "speech expression, a saying." Laotsu having, in one sentence, used this sign in two different senses, nearly all translators have suffered themselves to be misled. The sentence is as simple as

possible, and in two of my Chinese editions the commentators put "spoken," and: "by word of mouth." But of all the sinologues only Wells Williams has translated this sentence well, namely thus "The Tao which can be expressed is not the eternal Tao." Although the construction of the phrase is not accurately rendered, at any rate Williams has grasped the meaning.

After my work had already appeared in the periodical *De Gids*, I saw for the first time Professor de Groot's work "Jaarlijksche feesten en gebruiken der Emoy Chineezen," from which I gathered that he agreed with me in so far as to say also that "Tao" was untranslatable—a sub-lying conception "for which the Chinese philosopher himself could find no name, and which he consequently stamped with the word 'Tao.'" Professor de Groot adds: "If one translates this word by 'the universal soul of Nature,' 'the all-pervading energy of nature,' or merely by the word 'Nature' itself, one will surely not be far from the philosopher's meaning."

Although the term holds for me something still higher yet I find Professor de Groot's conception of it the most sympathetic of all those known to me.

5. This "Wu-Wei"—untranslatable as it is in fact—has been rendered by these sinologues into *"inaction"*—as though it signified idleness, inertia. It most certainly does not signify idleness, however, but rather action, activity—that is to say: "inactivity of the perverted, unnatural passions and desires," but "activity in the sense of natural movement proceeding from Tao." Thus, in the "Nan Hwa King" we find the following "The heavens and the earth do nothing" (in the evil sense "and" (yet) "there is nothing which they do not do." The whole of nature consists in "Wu-Wei," in natural, from-Tao-emanating movement. By translating Wu-Wei into "inaction" the sinologues have arrived at the exact opposite of the meaning of the Chinese text.

Laotsu himself does not dilate further upon the subject. What follows here is my own conception of the text. The whole first chapter of the original occupies only one page in the book, and contains only fifty-nine characters. It testifies to Laotsu's wonderful subtlety and terseness of language that he was able in so few words to say so much.

6. This sentence is translated from the "Tao-Teh-King" (chapter ii).

7. From the 56th chapter. This sentence is also to be found in 15th chapter of the "Nan Hwa King."

8. This runs somewhat as follows in the 6th chapter of the Nan Hwa King: "The true men of the early ages slept dreamlessly, and were conscious of self without care."

9.   This episode is translated from the 18th section of the "Nan Hwa King." By the "Great House" Chuang-Tse meant, of course, the universe, and this expression "house" lends to the passage a touch of familiar intimacy, showing Chuang-Tse to have the feeling that the dead one was well cared for, as though within the shelter of a house.—H. Giles, who renders it "Eternity," which does not appear at all in the Chinese text, loses by his translation the confiding element which makes Chuang-Tse's speech so touching. (Compare "Chuang Tsy," by H. Giles, London, Bernard Quaritch, 1889.) The actual words are "Ku Shih" = Great House.

10. In almost all the temples is a chamber in which the Mandarins lodge, and where Western travellers may usually stay for the night, and probably for longer periods.

11. The following, to the end of the sentence: "Poetry is the sound of the heart," has been translated by me from a preface by Ong Giao Ki to his edition of the Poetry of the Tang-Dynasty. Ong Giao Ki lived in the first half of the eighteenth century.

12   The Chinese do really preserve their treasures in this careful manner. It is usual for an antique figure of Buddha to lie in a silk-lined shrine, the shrine in a wooden chest, and the chest in a cloth. It is unpacked upon great occasions.

13. Such a figure as the above-described is not a mere figment of the author's imagination—such figures really exist. A similar one is in the possession of the author.

14. The Soul-Pearl "Durmâ."

15. The figure in the author's possession is by Tan Wei. Another great artist was Ho Chao Tsung, of certain figures by whom I have also, with very great trouble, become possessed. These names are well known to every artist, but I have endeavoured in vain to discover anything nearer with regard to them. They became famous after death; hut they had lived in such simplicity and oblivion, that now not even their birthplace is remembered. One hears conjectures, but I could arrive at no certainty.

HISTORICAL ESSAYS

by
DR. KIANG KANG-HU

THE BEGINNINGS OF
TAOIST PHILOSOPHY

The Taoists trace their original founder to the Yellow Emperor, and even to the Divine Farmer. They consider all the hermit philosophers under the Five Ti Rulers as of their school. Lu Shang, the prime minister of the first Chou emperor and the founder of the Ch'i state, who is commonly known as Chiang T'ai Kung, was also a Taoist sage. The extant teachings of these ancient sages is very ambiguous.

The real beginnings of Taoism begins with Laotzu, the Old Master. According to Su-ma-Ch'ien, the historian, who lived at the beginning of the First Century B. c., Laotzu was the official historian and custodian of the secret archives of the Cheu state. He was an older contemporary of Confucius and records a visit which Confucius paid him. He also tells of Laotzu's passing the guard at the frontier and writing the book.

History tells us that there were two more early Taoists in the Chou Dynasty. Lao Lai Tsu, a native of the Ch'u state, wrote a book of fifteen chapters which has been lost. Another Taoist named Lao Tan, who was also a historian of the imperial house, lived in the same state. These three Taoist sages who lived 200 or more years apart, according to history, are commonly believed to be the same man, who by his wisdom had attained longevity. Because of this some modernist scholars question the very existence of Lao-tzu and ascribe everything to the Loa Tan, but the simpler and more probable solution of the confusion is to accept the historicity of all three, but to give the credit for the original writing to Laotzu and consider the others as able disciples and possibly editors. The book in its present form might not have been written until the Third

Century at about the time of Lao Tan for it was engraved on stone tablets soon after that time. It might even contain some of the verses by Lao Tan without detracting from the larger credit that belongs to Laotzu. There are a number of legends that have gathered about the name of Laotzu but which only serve to throw doubt upon his existence.

The Chinese character for Tao is difficult to translate. It is made up of two characters: *shau*, meaning to lead, or the head; and *hsing*, meaning to walk, or a trail. Tao, therefore, would carry the meaning of 'that which leads us to walk on trails.' From this comes the meaning, The Way, or The Path, and a second meaning, Law or Method. There is a third meaning, also, the Word, or to talk. Tao is one of the oldest and commonest words used in ancient Chinese literature. It was used long before the beginning of Taoist philosophy. The same word is also used in Confucian works and just as frequently. But it was the Taoists who generalized it and mystified it and brought it to mean, instead of a practical method for the conduct of life, the abstract and natural course of things, and the pure nature of the universe and of life.

Laotzu's conception of Tao is something formless, nameless, invisible, unspeakable. It exists from before the creation and will exist till after the dissolution of all things. It has neither beginning nor end; it never changes but witnesses and withstands all changes. Tao is the mother of all substances and is the motive of all movements. It is the only and the absolute law of the universe. Laotzu's conception of *teh* is, that it is the virtue of Tao, the original nature of Tao, and should, therefore, be practiced by all human beings. By following this primeval law and by living in a state harmonious with it, one would be following the true Way of life, which is *teh*. His view of the universe is expressed by the term, *Tsu-jan*, which means, 'by itself, so', that is, it is pure naturalism. Everything is what it is because of its own nature as it follows its natural course. Because of an endless chain of causes and effects and conditions it can not be otherwise. He did not believe in a personal God, nor even in supreme intelligence, nor in any final purpose. The universe is simply an ever flowing current. It moves by a certain force, in a certain direction, according to a certain formula, but with no fixed aim. His view of life is expressed by the term, *wu-wei*, which means, doing nothing, or inaction. The best thing one can do in life is to do nothing, or as near nothing as possible. One should reflect stimulating and responsive calls but must not go beyond this limit, nor take any part of the action from which he could be spared.

Laotzu was not an atheist but his conception of God and heaven is nothing more than nature. He is not an anarchist but his conception of government is to think according to people's thought and to treat them as little children. He was strongly opposed to war and to the resort to force in any form be it expressed by law or religious rites or social custom. He is the chief representative of the negative and passive phase of Chinese philosophy.

Next to Laotzu comes Chuangtsu who lived about a hundred years later. His given name was Chou, his surname was Nan Wha. He was a native of the Meng district now a part of Anhui. He was at one time an actuary of the Ch'i Yuan. Requested by the king of Ch'u to become a minister of state, he declined and retired to write a book of fifty-three chapters of which since the Han Dynasty only thirty-three survive. The book was canonized by the T'ang emperors and named, *Nan-wha Chen Ching*. It is the second most important of the Taoist classics. It is divided into three parts of which the first part, consisting of seven chapters, is the most important. One will find in it more profound ideas and more elaborate discussions than in Laotzu.

There are three other classics of importance. The Lieh Tsu, by Lieh Yu-kou of the Cheng state; Wen Tsu, by Chi-jan of the Yueh state; and Ken-sang Tsu, by a scholar of the Lu state. These are the five classics of Taoism. As to their authenticity there is some question. Wen-Tsu is the oldest and it contains more quotations from Laotzu than the others. These books, and others written before the Eastern Han Dynasty and before the beginnings of Taoism as a religion, are suitable as sources for the study of the philosophy of Taoism.

Taoists, and especially Laotzu and Chuangtsu, are exponents of ancient philosophy and are very passive and non-resistant. They have always been the most radical leaders of thought against the state religion based upon the teachings of Confucius, against any military supported government and against any social order built up on conventions. They have always advocated free thinking and free teaching and, in the early days, after the passing of the feudal age, opened a new era of Chinese civilization. All schools of philosophy of their day and thereafter, and this includes the Confucian, came under their influence. No philosopher however different his philosophy ever disputed the Taoist philosophy or its teachers. On the contrary, they all proclaimed in some measure to be derived from ancient Taoist teachings. Aside from the Taoist religion, the ancient Taoist teachings have had a very strong and permanent hold on Chinese life and thought both personal and collective. Taoist elements of thought lie at the basis of Chinese characteristics of patience, reserve, egotism, peacefulness, and contentment. Whether these characteristics are virtues or not, it is in these qualities that the Chinese characteristics and the Taoist teachings are identical. Though both Taoism and Confucianism have taught the same principles of Tao and *teh* with similar definitions in many respects, the Confucianists compared with the Taoists have taught a more positive and active presentation of them. The Confucianists emphasize human activities in forming civilization, while the Taoists advise merely a return to nature and an obedience to her laws. It is therefore the Confucian scholars of later days who have criticized Taoism as being a one-sided philosophy that is good only for retirement and is bad for government. Some Taoists have replied to this by saying that nature itself is evolution and is never at a standstill, and that their course is wiser because it falls in with nature instead of foolishly trying to change or expedite the natural process of things.

Laotzu's idea of a return to nature is, however, somewhat different from that. Laotzu advocates passivity because it is the safest position in which to undergo natural evolution; he advocates simplicity because it is the best attitude of mind to understand compliance. He depicts the cultivation of Tao and *teh* first in one's person, then in his family, then in his town, then in his state, and then in the whole world, which is the same order that Confucius taught in his Great Learning. Laotzu often discusses about government and state affairs. He uses the term 'the perfect Sage' frequently and by it generally refers to the ruler. By reviewing the glorious achievements of the early Han emperors who reigned according to Laotzu's understanding of the principle of Tao, we are convinced that the Taoist philosophy, though a negative philosophy, is not alone a philosophy for hermits.

TAOIST RELIGION

Religion is very different from philosophy, often it becomes quite opposite and yet it is carried on in its name and claims to be the original teaching. Sometimes this is caused by the inclusion of some alien elements, but in case of Taoism in China, from beginning to end it has been an indigenous faith. It took about 650 years from the time of Laotzu to its proclamation as a religion, to complete this transformation. The difference between Taoist philosophy and Taoist religion is so great that one can hardly find any connection; in fact, it is doubtful if there is any. All relations asserted by modern Taoists are uncertain and unreliable. The transformation, however, can be traced.

After the passing of the early Taoist teachers, its teachings were invaded and finally dominated by believers in the 'two forces' and the 'five elements' (male and female; earth, water, fire, air, ether) . From these two schools emerged. The first, the Ch'an Wei School, became mixed up with a Confucian school and gave birth to witchcraft. The second, the Shen Hsien School, was dominated by adepts in discerning the 'wind and water influence (*fang-shih*)' who practiced alchemy and the art of prolonging life. The first emperor of the Ch'in Dynasty fell a victim to these adepts and sent out emissaries to seek for this elixir of life. In the Western Han Dynasty the chief counsel of its founder, Chang Liang, was fond of this doctrine, and the Emperor Wu-ti particularly favored it and made several unsuccessful attempts to find the philosopher's stone.

Under Emperor Kuang-wu of the Eastern Han Dynasty, in 34 A.D., Chang Tao-lin was born. It was by him that the Taoist religion was founded. He was a native of Chekiang Province although he spent

114

most of his life in the Dragon-tiger mountain in Kang-si, where he lived and taught to an extremely old age; he spent a great deal of his time in meditation and lived to be 123 years of age.

A century elapsed. Then came the revolution of the Yellow Turbans who were followers of Chang Tao-lin and whose leader was a descendant of him. The revolution was soon suppressed but the religion continued and spread among the lower classes. Chang Tao-lin who had been called, "the Divine Teacher," was later honored by having this title (Tien-shih) made hereditary. This Taoist papacy still continues with its seat in the Dragon-tiger mountains. In the Western Chin Dynasty two independent adepts appeared (Ke-hung and Tao Hung-thing) who were famous for their wisdom and magical achievements. Later another Heavenly Teacher appeared during the Northern Wei Dynasty, in North China who was highly regarded by the Tartar Emperors. This man was K'ou Ch'ien-chieh of Chili, and through his influence Taoism became established for a time as a state religion. It was during this time (440 A.D.) that Buddhism was persecuted and *Confucianism* was neglected.

Since the founding of the T'ang Dynasty, owing to the fact that its founder claimed to be a descendant of Laotzu, Taoist philosophy and the Taoist religion have been highly honored and promoted. The Old Master, Laotzu, was honored and his four great disciples; many Taoist priests were summoned to court and placed in high government positions. In the beginning of the Northern Sun Dynasty, Ch'ien T'uan and Ting Shao-wei, two great Taoist scholars, were honored by both Emperors T'ai Tzu and T'ai Tsung. Ch'ien T'uan's philosophy had a strong influence over Confucianism, and was directly the foundation of the so-called orthodox school of Taoism. Emperor Huei Tsung of the same Dynasty was a renowned patron of Taoism. He was often called the Taoist King. He regulated the Taoist priesthood into twenty-six ranks and two high priests were made ministers of state. He even went so far as to order all Buddhists to become Taoists. This was in 1119. It was during this revival of Taoism that meditation (ch'u zan ch'un) was revived. The first

Mongol Emperor Kublai confirmed the Taoist papacy, and made Chang Tsung-yen, the thirty-sixth generation from Chang Tao-lin, a member of the hereditary nobility (1275) .

In the Ming Dynasty a famous Taoist named Chang San-feng was summoned by the Emperor many times but never responded. Emperor Chia Ching in his long reign (1522-1566) devoted much attention to Taoist affairs and ordered Taoist sacrificial feasts throughout the Empire. Since the Ming Dynasty there has been a bureau in the central government to administer Taoist affairs, together with a similar Buddhist bureau. The Ch'ing Dynasty followed this system and made the heir of Chang Tao-lin, its honorary chief, an official of the fourth rank. The Chang family have thus enjoyed hereditary rank second only to the family of Confucius.

In modern times there have been two great branches of Taoist teachings, the Cheng Yi and the Ch'uan Chen. The former is the orthodox sect and follows strictly Chang Tao-lin's religious practices. Each of the two branches is again divided into two schools. The two schools of the orthodox branch are called Fu-lu and K'e Chiao, and are both under the Papacy that had been founded in 1161 in the Ch'in Dynasty. The First Patriarch of the first orthodox school was Lu Tung-pin, a retired Chin-shih scholar of the T'ang Dynasty. They practice witchcraft and most acts of exorcism and necromancy are under this sect; they use cryptic monograms, charms, spells, amulets in their services, and produce various psychic phenomena. The ouija board was their invention and its name originated in Fukien. It is called Fu-chi in Mandarin. The second Orthodox school, the Ke Ch'iao, confine their attention to the study of forms and rites and the practice of medicine. They are also interested in Taoist literature and ceremonies which have been developed mainly after Buddhist patterns and their costumes and ceremonies are often decorative and graceful.

The first of the heterodox schools is called the Lien Yang, or Chen Yang, and is devoted to the practice of physical and mental hygiene. They believe in strengthening the body and mind as a means of prolonging life and developing the spirit. This is achieved by secret meditations and exchange of vibrations. The Fang Chung Shu method for developing inner character, and the science of 'sexual' transformations (a secret and cryptic word for the positive and negative principles) are important elements of their practices. The second of the heterodox schools is called the Fu-shih and their interests are related to the science of medicine and alchemy. They think that the life elements of the human body can be supplied either by herbal nourishment or by mental and spiritual sublimations. They value lead and mercury as means for transmuting into gold and in making an elixir of immortality. Most of these schools have northern and southern divisions. In general the Northern are more materialistic, the Southern more idealistic and less formal. *

As stated above, the Taoist religion is an abuse of Taoist philosophy. We find nothing essentially in common between them and, in many

---

*   Besides these strictly Taoist sects, there are minor sects that are often more Buddhistic than Taoist, that practice meditation and are more spiritual and sincere. Most of these derive from Yuen Dynasty Ch'u-San-chen. Among these is the Eternal Life Sect that originated at the close of the Ming Dynasty in Chekiang Province under the leadership of Chan-sung-tao (Wang Chansung) as their first patriarch. This is an eclectic sect recognizing Buddha, Laotzu, and Confucius, as of equal merit. They are generally found in mountain temples living as small communistic Brotherhoods with their lay members living in the surrounding villages. They practice meditation and are very industrious, celibate, earnest and friendly.

     As a religion Taoism passed over into Japan and became mixed up with Japanese history and legends to make up Japanese Shin-tao-ism, which, as it is involved with the cult of Emperor worship, is almost a state religion. In Korea it was the source of the T'ien Tao religion which has exercised a strong influence over political and social life. In the present Republic of China, Confucianism has been made a kind of state religion, but the rising of different sects integrating the 'three religions', such as the Tao Yuan, T'ung Shan She, and others, and a renaissance of a more spiritual Buddhism among the laity, is an indication of the undercurrent power of the old Tao conception.

respects, they are conflicting. This is especially so between Laotzu's teachings and the orthodox Papacy. The true nature of the Taoist religion is a combination of the ancient animism, spiritism, mythology, and the popular superstitions of the day. Its formulation was chiefly influenced by imperial encouragement of the adepts and the social adoption of Buddhism. From the ancient animism and Buddhism, Chang Tao-lin made up the Taoist religion just as Mohammed made up Islam from early Judaism and Christianity. They both borrowed foreign faiths and conformed them to native ideas to suit their own purpose. Against Laotzu's atheistic tendency the Taoist religion created numerous divinities. Against his disapproval of names and forms, it manufactured voluminous scriptures, rituals and elaborate ceremonials. Against his belief in the simple quiet life it imitated the ranks and standards of nobles and officials. Misunderstanding and ignoring Laotzu's warning against greed and lust, many Taoist practices of alchemy and sexual 'gravitation' appeared disguised in secret teachings and cryptic terms. On the other hand, the Taoist religion borrowed from the Buddhists the conception of the 'three bodies' of Buddha, but interpreted it as meaning their ancient belief in the 'three purities':—Virility (*Ching*), Air (*Ch'i*), and Spirit (*Shen*). It enumerated the eight immortals and the twenty-eight star gods, and pictured the heavens and hells after the Buddhist tales, and they have adopted the Buddhist practice of saying masses for the dead.

Differing somewhat from the Buddhists many orthodox Taoist priests forsake their temples and brotherhoods to marry and live the ordinary life of the world. Taoists often use their surnames and wear long hair. There are none or very few Taoist nuns. During the change of Dynasties, particularly between the Ming and Ch'ing, many officials, soldiers and scholars refused to submit to Manchu customs and became Taoists, because they were the only ones who were allowed to keep old Chinese ways and wear long hair. Strangely enough, during the recent revolution, the Taoists were the last to lay aside their queues.

The influence of the Taoist religion in China is neither as strong as the influence of Buddhism or, the Taoist philosophy, but all the popular superstitions, practices and resort to geomantic magic, including spiritism and shamanism, can be regarded as Taoist in some form. The many revolutions of the Ch'ing Dynasty, besides the T'ai P'ing Christian and Mohammedan, were all connected more or less closely with the Taoist sects. Taoism has never created any great literature or art, as Buddhism and Confucianism has; it has never been the religion of the intellectual classes and has always been looked down upon by the literati.

CPSIA information can be obtained
at www.ICGtesting.com
Printed in the USA
LVHW080957160820
663323LV00015B/461

9 781374 874947